JET PROVOST BOYS

True Tales From the Operators of the Jet Provost and Strikemaster

JET PROVOST BOYS

True Tales From the Operators of the Jet Provost and Strikemaster

DAVID WATKINS

GRUB STREET | LONDON

Published by
Grub Street
4 Rainham Close
London SW11 6SS

Copyright © Grub Street 2023
Copyright text © David Watkins 2023

A CIP record for this title is available from the British library

ISBN-13: 978-1-911667-44-5

All rights reserved. No part of this publication may be reproduced, stored in a retrieval system, or transmitted in any form or by any means electronic, mechanical, photocopying, recording or otherwise, without the prior permission of the copyright owner.

Design by Myriam Bell Design, UK

Printed and bound by Finidr, Czech Republic

CONTENTS

Foreword 6
Introduction and Acknowledgements 8
CHAPTER ONE: All-Through Jet Training is Here to Stay 16
CHAPTER TWO: The Jet Provost T Mk 4 – Higher and Faster 46
CHAPTER THREE: Jet Provost Mk 5 – The MG Sports Car of the Skies 68
CHAPTER FOUR: Lesser-Known Jet Provost Operators 87
CHAPTER FIVE: Random Jet Provost Memories 105
CHAPTER SIX: Foreign Sales 117
CHAPTER SEVEN: The BAC Strikemaster 138
APPENDIX 1: Strikemaster Production at Warton 167
APPENDIX 2: Jet Provost/Strikemaster Design Projects 168
Glossary 170
Select Bibliography 172
Index 173

FOREWORD

SQN LDR TERRY LLOYD

In his previous book *From Jet Provost to Strikemaster* David provides detailed information on the Jet Provost with its evolution in the 1950s from the Piston Provost leading to the Strikemaster and the several variants in between.

In this book he has collected the reminiscences from many of the pilots who flew the aircraft both in the training and operational roles. These stories show

Terry Lloyd (in the cockpit) with BAC senior production test pilot, Pete Ginger, at the side of aircraft on the day of departure from Warton of the first two Strikemasters to Kenya on 5 January 1971. (BAC)

how popular the aircraft was: basic training, formation aerobatic teams, leading on to the Strikemaster used in both training and in operations most notably those in Oman during the Dhofar War.

I flew the Jet Provost at RAF Syerston way back in 1960, it was my first instructional role albeit I had completed my instructors course at CFS on the Piston Provost. Next was Central Flying School where I was fortunate to join the 1963 team as No. 6 and then in 1964 as leader of the Red Pelicans which was the RAF premier team of that year.

In 1969 I joined the Kenyan air force on loan service and flew one of the first two Strikemasters from Warton to KAF Eastleigh. My next and final association with the aircraft was in the Sultanate of Oman when I joined No. 1 Squadron at Masirah in 1983.

I found the pilots' stories, many of whom I know, made interesting reading and highlighted just how versatile the Jet Provost and its variants proved to be.

For me the book was a trip down memory lane and I am sure all who read this will better understand how well regarded the aircraft was and of course will thoroughly enjoy the many 'war stories'.

Sqn Ldr Terry Lloyd joined the RAF in August 1954 and completed his flying training in Canada. Between 1957 and 1958 he flew Canberras with No. 6 Squadron in Cyprus, before qualifying as a QFI in 1960. Following a brief tour instructing at No. 2 FTS, he joined the CFS Staff at RAF Little Rissington and has the distinction of leading the RAF's only Jet Provost premier aerobatic display team in 1964.

INTRODUCTION AND ACKNOWLEDGEMENTS

With the advent of turbo-powered jet aircraft, it soon became apparent that training aircraft fitted with appropriate engines would be required to enable future generations of pilots to be made familiar with the necessary handling characteristics. The previous Provost/Vampire pilot training sequence had proved to be relatively successful, but by February 1957 the results of the evaluation courses conducted at RAF Hullavington clearly demonstrated the suitability of the Hunting Percival Jet Provost basic trainer as the logical step in providing pupils with their entire flying instruction on jet aircraft. Although this had been considered for some time, the 'Hullavington Experiment' also showed a 'significant' saving of flying hours during the advanced phase of their training and an overall saving on the complete wings course.

Coinciding with the announcement, the Secretary of State for Air confirmed that the RAF had decided to adopt the Jet Provost as its standard ab initio/basic trainer and that a production order had been placed with the manufacturers for an initial batch of 100 aircraft, with deliveries to RAF Flying Training Command beginning in the summer of 1959. Eager to promote the new jet trainer, the RAF placed numerous glossy adverts in the various aviation journals, magazines and newspapers during the late 1950s and early 1960s, which focused upon the glamour and the excitement of young men eager to join the RAF for a career which included flying the Jet Provost.

Many of these aspirants would not only experience their first taste of jet flying in the Jet Provost but also be a part of the innovative 'all-through' jet-flying training sequence, designed to radically transform the RAF's flying training syllabus and

INTRODUCTION AND ACKNOWLEDGEMENTS

be subsequently adopted by many leading air forces.

Although the designation 'Jet Provost' had been used on a semi-official basis for some time, the name was finally sanctioned for production aircraft on 3 June 1957 by the Air Council Standing Committee, headed by Mr George Ward:

"In July, 1953, I agreed as ACCS (OR), that the ten development trainers converted from the Provost should be called 'Jet Provosts'. A Nomenclature Notice was originally issued giving the official designation as 'Jet Provost T. Mark 1'. I felt at the time as these aircraft were only for trial purposes, we did not need to consider re-naming them officially unless and until a production order in quantity was placed. We have reached that situation and I would appreciate the Standing Order's views as to whether we should give a new name to the production Jet Provosts.

Two examples of the adverts placed in contemporary magazines during the 1960s designed to attract young men for a career in the RAF. (Mod PR)

"It has been suggested that during the changeover period when there are considerable numbers of Provosts and Jet Provosts in service together, ambiguity may arise, particularly in respect of engineering and supply aspects. On the other hand, the existing name 'Jet Provost' had been very widely publicised both inside and particularly outside the services and the aircraft is known by this name in potential overseas markets. We have had the Mark 1 Jet Provosts in service for nearly two years and, to my knowledge, this similarity in name has not caused any major difficulty or confusion. A minor consideration also is that Hunting Percival have produced all their production drawings under the name of Jet Provost T. Mark 3 and all these will have to be changed if we rename the aircraft. I feel that the well-known name of Jet Provost should be retained, the various types being distinguished by mark numbers."

Despite the endless changes to RAF pilot training policy between 1959 and 1989, the versatile and undemanding Jet Provost established itself not only as a basic trainer, but also in the navigation, refresher, forward air control and 'clockwork mice' roles. Its simple and uncomplicated handling qualities also soon proved the Jet Provost to be popular as a mount with display teams and despite its limitations, virtually every RAF jet-flying training school produced an informal team to entertain those attending the numerous flying events between 1958 and 1976. Although not always well received by the station or its engineers as it meant extra work and a diversion of resources, these events included national and international air shows – from major NATO displays, Battle of Britain 'At Home' Days to local garden fetes, each of which enhanced national prestige and the service's public image. Sadly, the impact of the fuel crisis and the drastic defence cuts of the 1970s brought an end to these varied and original routines by the RAF Jet Provost display teams, leaving spectators with individual contributions by pilots provided by their respective units or, latterly, by privately owned aircraft on the 'Warbird' air show circuit.

While the Jet Provost continued to serve in its training capacity, trials with the BAC 167 counter-insurgency aircraft (COIN)/light-attack model of the Jet Provost Mk 5 were steadily progressing, with the prototype making its maiden flight from Warton on 26 October 1967. To find a name for the new aircraft a competition came up with 'Strikemaster', which was officially endorsed in October 1968. A total of 150 airframes were eventually built at Warton to varying standards, offering a dual-role capability to the air forces of emergent nations and featuring an uprated Viper engine of 3,410 lbs thrust and four underwing pylons capable

INTRODUCTION AND ACKNOWLEDGEMENTS

of carrying bombs or rocket launchers on stressed wings. In August 1968, Saudi Arabia became the first country to receive its initial order for 25 Strikemaster Mk 80s, and by the time the last airframe rolled off the production line in 1983, a further ten overseas air forces had purchased the type.

Eventually, 700 Jet Provost and Strikemaster airframes were built at Luton and Warton, and those sold to foreign air arms would experience limited ground-attack operations in border disputes and internal warfare in Ceylon, Ecuador, Nigeria, Sudan, South Yemen and Venezuela; whether it was desert or jungle operations, both aircraft proved to be reliable and effective. In July 1972, the Strikemaster aircraft of the SOAF's Strike Wing proved to be no exception, having played a crucial part during the Dhofar War in Oman when 300 heavily-armed insurgents attacked the town of Mirbat, garrisoned with nine SAS and 30 Omani soldiers. During three hours of bloody fighting, two successive pairs of SOAF Strikemasters from Salalah responded to a call for help with both low-level gun and rocket attacks, which successfully repulsed the enemy fighters and resulted in a significant turning point in the conflict; some of the story of this largely forgotten campaign is faithfully recalled in this book by those who were involved in The Secret War, to whom I am most grateful.

Throughout its service career the Jet Provost attracted a variety of personal and conflicting opinions from aircrew, which ranged from: "My introduction to the Jet Provost Mk 3 did not generate a morsel of enthusiasm or devotion then or at any time thereafter" to "I loved flying the Jet Provost. Both the Mk 3 and Mk 5 were easy to fly. It was what the QFIs demanded of you that sorted the men from the boys."

But it was aviation journalist **Chris Long** who encapsulated the feelings of many other student pilots:

> "I was one of a very lucky group who started flying training at RAFC Cranwell on the Jet Provost 3 – so the first solo ever was on a jet. We completed our training to wings on a mix of the Mk 3 and Mk 4 to a total of 170 hours. I didn't come back to the Jet Provost until eight years later. After a short ground tour I was introduced to the Mk 5A on the refresher flying squadron (RFS) prior to Central Flying School to do the instructor course. I had enjoyed the aircraft and the role so much on RFS that I campaigned to get back to RFS for my instructional tour – fantastic. Next was a tour with the French air force before I met up with the Strikemaster in Saudi Arabia for nearly three years. So how did they shape up? I have a soft spot for the

> Mk 3 – nobody forgets their first solo, and the Mk 4 was pretty much the same. The Strikemaster was interesting because, fitted with four underwing fuel tanks, it had a much better range for the low-level training over the desert. But for sheer fun the Mk 5A was the best bet – only 50 minutes at low level, but it trundled around the UK at a comfortable 300 knots."

There were also the critics who had remarked on the failure rate of students following their ab-initio training; it was said that the Jet Provost was too easy to fly while the Provost was much more of a challenge, and this conjecture was supported by the remarkably high rate (50%-plus) of suspension from training on Provosts at Ternhill compared to that on Jet Provosts at Syerston. The result was that the less-able students who had passed the Syerston course were unable to cope with the Vampire and inevitably suspended, thus incurring a waste of public funds. The answer was to introduce 'streaming' and by 1960 all students completed the basic phase on the Jet Provost and, depending on how well they had performed – and the RAF's requirements at the time – they moved on to the advanced phase on the Gnat, Varsity or helicopters.

Wg Cdr Jeff Jefford:

> "Prior to the 1960s everyone did the whole 250-hour(ish) Prentice/Harvard, later Provost/Vampire Flying Training sequence, so that all pilots reached a common (notionally potential fighter pilot) standard before gaining their wings – only then were they streamed onto mini-jets or heavies. In the early 1960s the streaming decision had been brought forward to the end of the 120-hour basic Jet Provost phase. In the 1980s the decision was made even earlier – halfway through the basic phase. The motivation, in both cases, was economy. In earlier times, it would have been possible to give a slow runner who, it was thought might still make the grade, another discretionary five hours or so to see if it made a difference. That sort of flex became increasingly scarce as time went by. If you failed one of the various progress tests that cropped up during the course – your number was pretty much up. I was snagged on just such a check ride at the 80-hour point. I flew just once more – a check-ride with the squadron commander – and that was it."

A further round of 'streaming' aircrew students in the 1980s coincided with a move to replace the RAF's Jet Provosts with a more economical aircraft, which

INTRODUCTION AND ACKNOWLEDGEMENTS

resulted in Air Staff Target (AST) 412 being issued in June 1984 for a more low-cost training aircraft. The CFS preferred a turbo-prop basic trainer, and felt that a trainer with high torque from the engine would be a more challenging aircraft, together with being more economic than a pure jet. A number of designs were considered, with the leading contender for the contract being the Embraer/Short Tucano, which was declared the winner and officially announced in Parliament by the Secretary of State for Defence, Michael Heseltine, in March 1985.

Following a lengthy assessment by the CFS, the Tucano gradually replaced the Jet Provosts at No. 7 Flying Training School (FTS) at Church Fenton in December 1988, followed by No. 3 FTS at Cranwell and No. 1 FTS at Linton-on-Ouse. Destined to be the final unit to operate the Jet Provost, No. 6 FTS, which was tasked with navigator training at Finningley, saw the progressive replacement by the Tucano from September 1992 and the adoption of the Hawk for advanced tactical flying. The Jet Provosts were finally withdrawn from No. 6 FTS in September 1993.

Following their retirement from RAF service, a large number of Jet Provost airframes were relegated for ground-training purposes at RAF Halton, Cosford and St Athan, employed for crash-rescue training, museum exhibits, or resold to private buyers. In early March 2019, the end finally came when the remaining Jet Provost Mk 5A airframes, XW320, XW327, XW375 and XW436, were retired from the Defence College of Aeronautical Engineering at Cosford, where they had been used to train aircraft engineers for all three services; the airframes were later put up for disposal and sold in early 2020, while XW327 was retained for emergency-rescue training.

The contents of this book are not intended to repeat all the information contained in the original edition of *From Jet Provost to Strikemaster*, but to complement it with additional material and untold stories I received following its publication. Therefore, I am most grateful to those who contributed their anecdotes, information and previously unseen images; your infinite patience and first-hand accounts provided the integrity for me to complete this work.

I am especially grateful to Kate Yates for her extremely generous support with my continuous photographic requirements. Also to Candy and Polly Foster for providing me with the valuable background to the service career of their father, the late Richard 'Dick' Foster; Jill Harris and John Drinkell for kindly responding to me with information and selected pages from the logbook of Sqn Ldr W.G. 'Bill' Drinkell DFC AFC; Air Cdre Jim Barclay AFC RNZAF for permission to extract information on the Strikemaster from his personal diary; and to Sqn Ldr Terry Lloyd for kindly agreeing to write the foreword.

My gratitude is also extended to the following: Alan Allen, Sqn Ldr Tim Allen, Andy Anderson, James Baldwin, Ian Bashall, Laurie Bean, Jeff Bell, Air Cdre J.A. 'Tinkle' Bell OBE FBIM, Chris Blower RN, Sqn Ldr Roy Booth, Alex Brancaccio, Derick Bridge, Sqn Ldr Rod Brown, Jim Burns, Mike Butt, Bruce Byron, Steve Carr, Dudley Carvell, Rob Chambers, Wg Cdr Sean Chiddention MBE, Dave Coldicutt, Sqn Ldr Allan Corkett, Cdre Bill Covington CBE RN (Retd), Dave Croser, Peter Curtin, Wg Cdr Eddie Danks, Paul Dandeker, Charles Davies (Strikemaster 72), John Davy, Richard Dawe, Ray Deacon, Rod Dean, Tony Doyle, Lt Cdr David Eagles RN, Gp Capt Mike Edwards AFC, Gp Capt Tom Eeles BA FRAeS, Diogo Eira, Sqn Ldr Eric Evers, Capt (Mrs) Ashi Fernando, Sqn Ldr Chira Fernando RCyAF (retd), Keith Gainey, Peter Gardiner, Norman Giffin, Norman Gill, Mark Gilson, Y.K. Goh, John Grainge, Wg Cdr Dennis 'Nobby' Grey for his permission to extract material from his personal account of SOAF operations, Anthony Haig-Thomas, Brian Hall, Ian Halwood, Steven Hand, Sqn Ldr John Harvey, Ian Hawkridge, Leif Hellstrom, Wg Cdr P.J. 'Curly' Hirst, Peter Hoar, Barry Hobkirk, Stan Hodgkins, Dave Horsfield, Gp Capt Brian Hoskins AFC FRAeS, Stevie Howard, Capt Bill Jago, Wg Cdr 'Jeff' Jefford, Peter Jennings, David Jones, Gp Capt Martin 'Dim' Jones, Michael Kelly, Jukka Keränen, Richard King, Gp Capt Kumar Kirinde (retd) SLAF, Ares Klootwyk, Wg Cdr Olly Knight, K. Sree Kumar, Danny Lavender (Courtesy of Caroline Lavender), Stewart Lenton, Sqn Ldr Noel Lokuge, Chris Long, Bill Macgillivray, Erik Mann, Gp Capt Vijay Mayadev, David McCann, Keith McCloskey/Alistair Henderson, Andy Marden, Kris Muthukrishnan, Don McClen, Gp Capt Paul McDonald, Dave McIntyre, Larry Milberry/Canav Books, David Milne-Smith, Mike Napier, Terry Nash, Brett Nicholls, Alick Nicholson, Bob Osborne, Ken Parry, Ron Pattinson, Sqn Ldr Russell Peart AFC (for his kind permission to extract information on the Harabut and Haif incidents from his book *From Lightnings to MiGs*), Dondi Pesquera, Mark Petrie, AVM Les Phipps CB AFC, Jagan Pillarisetti, Patrick Vinot Prefontaine, Air Cdre Richie Profit OBE AFC MRAeS, Rob Ricketts, Hugh Rigg, Sqn Ldr John Robinson AFC*, Peter Rolt, Wg Cdr Mick Ryan, David Sargent, Rod Sargent, Mike Sedman, AVM Sir John Severne KCVO OBE AFC DL, Brian Shadbolt, Alan, Sheppard, Ian Sheppard, Tim Simpson, Lt Cdr Hugh Slade RN, AVM Chris Spence RAAF, Steve Stanton, Mark Stephenson, Reg Stock, VAdm Sir Jonathan Tod KCB CBE RN, Bob Thompson FRAeS, Air Cdre Tim Thorn

INTRODUCTION AND ACKNOWLEDGEMENTS

AFC FRAeS, Rob Turner, AM Pattathil Venugopal, David Warren, Alex Weitz, Rupert Weitz, Rowland White, Joe Whitfield, Keith Wilson-Clark, and Wg Cdr Ian 'Iggy' Wood RNZAF.

I also would like to extend my thanks to all those at Grub Street, in particular John Davies and Natalie Parker, for all their hard work in making this project possible.

As usual, every attempt has been made to identify and acknowledge the original owners of the images used in this book. In some cases, this has not been entirely possible and I therefore hope that I will be forgiven if your work was considered to be entirely suitable to accompany this history. Thank you!

David Watkins
April 2023

CHAPTER ONE

ALL-THROUGH JET TRAINING IS HERE TO STAY

The association of the Percival Aircraft Company with military pilot training had dated from the end of the Second World War when it was successful in meeting the requirement for the RAF's first post-war basic trainer, the P.40 Prentice. This was followed by the P.56 Provost, built in equally large numbers which entered service as the RAF's standard basic trainer in May 1953. It soon proved a popular aircraft and subsequently became the first half of the RAF's Provost/Vampire training sequence the following September.

The close collaboration between the manufacturer and RAF Flying Training Command had placed the company in a favourable position to evaluate the introduction of an all-jet training syllabus, a concept which was considered to remove the inconsistent step from piston-engined to jet-powered aircraft types.

In April 1951, a design study was made at Luton with the object of producing a jet-powered training variant of the Provost as the logical step in which a service pilot would be taught to fly entirely on a turbo-powered training aircraft. The following August, Hunting took the decision to proceed with such a project on a private-venture basis, and to ensure that it could be built and flown in the shortest possible time it was proposed to use as many standard components as practicable, including the wings, tail surfaces and undercarriage legs.

The Hunting Percival P.84 Jet Provost basic jet-trainer project attracted the interest of the Air Ministry, and on 24 March 1953 the Secretary of State for Air, Mr George Ward, showed his support for the project when he announced in the House of Commons that he had signed a contract with the company, worth £85,000, for an initial batch of ten pre-production Jet Provost T Mk 1s (XD674–XD680 and XD692–XD694) with an additional airframe – G-AOBU – included for use as a company demonstrator.

The prototype Jet Provost T Mk 1, XD674, made its first, uneventful, flight at Luton during the evening of 26 June 1954 by the company chief test pilot, R.G. 'Dick' Wheldon. Further proving flights were made over the next few days and, despite an unfortunate wheels-up landing on 18 July, it was quickly repaired and made its debut at the Farnborough SBAC Show in September.

In May 1955, initial deliveries to the RAF began when Jet Provost Mk 1, XD677 was delivered to the RAF Handling Squadron at Manby, followed by two further aircraft (XD676 and XD679) being issued to the CFS (Basic) at RAF South Cerney in July 1955. Tasked with the initial evaluation and compilation of a basic training syllabus for the first stage of the official service trials – Phase 'A' – the CFS team at South Cerney included Sqn Ldr W.G. 'Bill' Drinkell, Flt Lts John W. Morrice and David Houser.

XD674, being prepared for its first flight at Luton on 26 June 1954. (BAe Systems Heritage Warton-Percival/Hunting Collection)

Former wartime Bomber Command pilot, Sqn Ldr Bill Drinkell had gained his wings at Pensacola, Florida, and later flew on the Berlin Airlift and in Japan. In March 1950, he qualified as an instructor at Little Rissington and was posted to RAF Heany, in Southern Rhodesia. Between August 1954 and December 1955, he instructed primarily on the Hunting Provost at CFS (Basic), South Cerney, and was also a member of the official service evaluation team which completed the original trials of the Jet Provost Mk 1.

Bill Drinkell's first flight in a Jet Provost was on 28 July 1955 with 'Sqn Ldr Cooke', followed by a number of familiarisation and conversion trips with fellow instructors. By the time he completed his last sortie (an air test) he had flown 15.08 hours on the Jet Provost out of the total of 111 hours achieved by the team during the evaluation at South Cerney. In January 1956 he was posted to Rashid to resume his instructional duties with the Royal Iraqi Air Force.

The evaluation was completed by the end of August 1955, allowing the aircraft to join the other pre-production Jet Provosts at No. 2 FTS, RAF Hullavington,

Jet Provost T Mk 1s of No. 2 FTS at Hullavington in 1957. (BAe Systems Heritage Warton-Percival/Hunting Collection)

taking part in Phase 'B' of the experimental training programme, where the first ten instructors were also converted.

The commanding officer of No. 2 FTS/CFS (Basic) between October 1953 and May 1956 was Wg Cdr O.L. Gilson. He was also involved in the official Jet Provost service trials at RAF South Cerney and Hullavington in 1955, and the extracts from his logbook are typical of some of the work undertaken by the CFS team during this period:

22 July 1955: Jet Provost XD679 – Mr Wheldon/Self – Delivery to South Cerney
30 July 1955: Jet Provost XD679 – Self/Sqn Ldr Drinkell – General handling – Aerobatics
6 August 1955: Jet Provost XD679 – Self/Sqn Ldr Drinkell – Landings at Hullavington
8 August 1955: Jet Provost XD679 – Self/Flt Lt Morrice – High-Level Aerobatics

No. 2 FTS had transferred from Northern Ireland to Hullavington in June 1954, equipped with Hunting Percival Provosts for the basic training of student pilots. By 1955, the school was commanded by Gp Capt R.J. Abrahams OBE, and had been selected with the task of evaluating all-through jet training with an experimental 45-week/160 flying hours course for students on Hunting Percival Jet Provost Mk 1s. The first two aircraft (XD676 and XD677) of an eventual eight were delivered to the separate 'F' Flight – or 'Jet Flight' – in August 1955, commanded by Flt Lt John Evans. The following month, 18 acting pilot officers were transferred from OCTU at Kirton-in-Lindsey to become the first intake of students to join No. 113 (Jet) Course; ten of which had never flown before and eight had some previous flying experience with various university air squadrons, air training corps or private flying clubs.

Flying training began by the end of September, with Plt Off John Jackson becoming the first student to solo on the Jet Provost on 13 October 1955 (in XD677), followed by Plt Off Richard 'Dick' Foster four days later (in XD680); although Jackson had managed to solo after seven hours and 15 minutes of dual instruction, he had already flown 150 hours on Chipmunk and Harvard aircraft with the RAFVR, while Foster made RAF history by becoming the first to reach solo standard on jet aircraft after eight hours and 20 minutes without any previous flying experience. By the end of October all the students had flown solo although, in spite of their success in reaching the solo stage, not all maintained a satisfactory rate of progress, with five being suspended, including one with persistent airsickness.

Candy Foster:

"In October 1955, Dick Foster was one of 18 'guinea pigs' in the first ab-initio jet-training experiment, and completed the course with a trophy for winning the aerobatic display. A rather amusing incident at the passing-out parade convinced him of the hypocrisy of the 'top brass' when, after watching the aerobatic display, the Secretary of State for Air asked him if the aeroplane could 'loop the loop'! Dick did his advanced training on Vampires at RAF Swinderby, and two years later his ambition to become a pilot came to fruition when he got his wings, qualifying as a Royal Air Force pilot in 1957."

Ian Sheppard was a student on the first course:

"I arrived at Hullavington on 2 September 1955 and went solo on 20 October after five hours and 45 minutes of training. I was very new to this sort of life and probably quite naive, so I did what I was told and toed the line, and really we were too busy to do much else. We all moaned (why else join the services?) but the chief gripe was – I think – the fact that our course was an experiment when the Jet Provost was actually being tried out to see if it was any good at its job. There was a great deal of PR stuff surrounding the whole thing, e.g. much was made of the cheapness of turbine fuel (referred to as paraffin) as against aviation petrol. Sundry visitors also arrived from home and overseas, so we regularly had to clean the windows, empty the ashtrays, polish the floor etc. and shake hands with whoever was put in front of us. We were, I think, dimly conscious that our wartime predecessors had a poor opinion of 'line-shooting' so we loyally said what a wonderful aircraft it was, what a good idea it was and so forth, and it rather went against the grain. And fancy asking a bunch of ab-initio students with a handful of flying hours what they thought of the aircraft – any aircraft!

"Richard Foster was an outspoken South African. He was also a very good pilot and first to go solo on the Jet Provost. He and I had the same instructor Flt Lt Ted Willey – an ex-Sunderland pilot. He was known as Richard 'F*****g' Foster, as the adjective was his most commonly used word. I can't remember what happened to him after Hullavington, but I think he was at Swinderby because I recall an occasion

First Jet Provost Course at Hullavington with APOs Alf Foster, Dick Foster (credited as the first solo on type in October 1955) and Ken Hart. (Air Ministry)

when the flight crew room contained, among others, some Rhodesians. They were bitching like mad about the awful weather, dreadful place etc. and Richard Foster shouted back: 'This may be the arsehole of the world but don't forget that you are only passing through it!'"

The progress of the initial course at Hullavington had been closely watched by representatives of several foreign air forces, and especially by the CFS Examining Wing which tested the student standard and assessed them as 'high average'. The subsequent report stated that:

"It reflects most favourably on the suitability of the aircraft as an ab-initio trainer. Compared to the average student the jet-trained student has, in a shorter time, achieved a more dexterous and better mental approach to the art of modern flying."

As a result of the CFS report, it was decided to transfer six pupils to RAF Swinderby to receive advanced training on the de Havilland Vampire. The remainder of the course were left behind to complete the Jet Provost syllabus, and although it had originally been intended to hold one evaluation course at Hullavington, it was subsequently considered possible to continue jet basic training at Hullavington with further courses to confirm and consolidate the results being attained.

Used extensively for engine development trials in 1955, XD694 eventually became a ground instructional air frame and preserved at RAF Cosford. (BAe Systems Heritage Warton-Percival/Hunting Collection)

Ian Sheppard again:

"Between late March and early April 1956, a small group of us were sent to RAF Swinderby for an experimental, advanced training course of 85 flying hours on the Vampire trainer to virtually solo standard. We then returned to Hullavington and completed the course on 25 April 1956."

Several interesting facts about the course soon appeared when it was found that no student failed to go solo, which in itself was a record, and those students with previous flying experience had taken eight-and-a-half hours dual to go solo, while complete beginners averaged 14 hours.

The second course began in July 1956 and was briefly joined by the prototype Jet Provost Mk 2 (XD694) in September for a comparative evaluation with the Mk 1, completing some 260 flying hours before transferring to Armstrong Siddeley for engine trials. As with the first course, most of the flying was carried out at nearby Keevil aerodrome, the relief landing ground for Hullavington. **James Baldwin** was a student on the second course:

"I went solo on 31 July 1956 in a Jet Provost Mk 1 XD675 at Hullavington. The course syllabus was almost completely based on that of the piston version, but the

ALL-THROUGH JET TRAINING IS HERE TO STAY

Mk 1 allowed a wider use of airspace, including flying at a higher altitude. I started flying on the Mk 1 and was one of the four students who later did a bit on the Mk 2, which was the first short undercarriage version of the aircraft, and we switched quite easily between both versions. When we were tested by the CFS Examining Wing it became obvious that we knew more about the aircraft than they did. Looking back, its handling was not too bad and aerobatics were not a problem, either. A certain amount of our flying was from the nearby airfield at Keevil but we did very little formation work because our course was cut back a bit. We were also very aware of the small fuel load and the limited range of the aircraft. It was early days for me but I enjoyed the experience and it was not until 50 years later that I flew a later variation of the 'beast' for 20 minutes with Tony Haig-Thomas to celebrate our first solo."

Despite a spate of undercarriage and engine failures, only one aircraft was written off when in August 1956, the engine of XD692 failed on approach during a routine practice force-landing and collided with a wall in a field near Tetbury; both crew members, Flt Sgt 'Jock' Naismith and Plt Off E.P. 'Ted' Kendall, were fortunately uninjured. As a result of similar incidents involving the aircraft's Armstrong Siddeley Viper engine flaming out from free fuel igniting in the rear fuselage under negative g, all aerobatic flying in Jet Provost T Mk 1s was banned until the following February. **Brian Shadbolt**:

"Ted Kendall was chopped fairly early in the course and went off to a navigation school with several others who failed to make the grade. I am surprised we didn't have more engine failures; it was after all a very short-life drone engine. It was also not uncommon on pre-flight checks to look in the jet pipe and find little metal balls which had once been turbine blades.

"On 2 August 1956, my instructor, Flt Lt Dick Tuffin flew with me in XD675. We did 25 minutes circuit bashing on the short runway at Hullavington. He then said, 'I'll do this landing,' and subsequently ran off the end onto the grass. 'Bloody pneumatic brakes!' he exclaimed. We parked on the taxiway and he hopped out and said: 'Try and do better than that!'"

With the apparent success of the evaluation, the Air Ministry made the decision in February 1957 to proceed with the 'all-through' jet-training sequence with the Jet Provost Mk 3 as soon as possible, and that the Ministry of Supply would place an order for "a sufficient number of Jet Provosts".

Following this announcement, a third 'all-through' course began at Hullavington in March 1957 as it was considered necessary to keep the present Jet Provost Flight to retain the instructional and servicing skills and provide additional student pilots with the necessary experience of jet-flying techniques. The official announcement also confirmed that the course would continue until "sufficient production aircraft became available". However, despite the delivery date for the new aircraft being subsequently amended to June 1959, the decision to continue with the third course was maintained and, despite poor serviceability and bad weather, the 12 students of No. 125 (Jet) Course eventually completed their basic flying training in November 1957.

DEVELOPMENT AND DEMONSTRATION AIRCRAFT

Meanwhile, work on four pre-production Jet Provost T Mk 2s had also been progressing at Luton. Jointly funded by Hunting and Armstrong Siddeley, the pre-production airframes included XD694, G-AOHD, G-23-1 and G-AOUS, which became part of the Hunting sales and development fleet by August 1958.

XD694 first flew in September 1955 and was involved in company test flying before being transferred to Boscombe Down for its service acceptance trials, which resulted with the incorporation of many refinements omitted by the manufacturer in the Mk 1. These improvements included a 1,750-lb thrust AS Viper 8 Mk 102 turbojet being installed in the Mk 2 version, which gave an extra 100 lbs of thrust. The Viper engine's slightly larger jet pipe necessitated a number of structural changes, which included a top 'beak' extension to the rear of the fuselage to avoid flow separation and buffeting, and a refinement of the fin and rudder with the replacement of the ventral fin with a dorsal extension leading into the fin. The hydraulic operation of flaps, brakes, undercarriage and airbrakes to substitute the original pneumatic system was also incorporated, while the long, stalky undercarriage legs of the Provost were replaced with much shorter units which retracted into the wings rather than the fuselage. Surprisingly, despite earlier criticism by the A&AEE, no provision had been made for the installation of ejection seats.

Of interest, during its time at Bitteswell due to the resurfacing of the runways from 13 July to 14 August 1956, several of the 'key' flight-test aircraft, including XD694 were transferred to continue their intensive flight-test programme from RAF Honiley. During this period, an incident occurred in the late afternoon of 21 November 1958. **Rod Sargent** continues the story.

G-AOHD at a demonstration in the facilities of Fabrica Militar de Aviones, Córdoba, Argentina during a tour of Latin American countries in August 1958. (Vladimiro Cettolo/Atilio Marino)

"On 21 November 1958, Harry Rayner in Gannet AS.1 WN345 took off at 1415 hrs on his second flight of the day on that aircraft. This was a Gannet Mk 1 modified to take the latest AS Double-Mamba test bed with the Gannet AEW.3 engine exhaust configuration. About 1430 hrs Harry reported that he had an undercarriage problem and returned to the Bitteswell circuit for a visual check on the aircraft. The main wheels were fully extended with the nose leg semi-retracted, and it was concluded that the nosewheel had retracted before the D-door opened and jammed.

The chief test pilot, 'Tom' Frost, hastily visited the control tower and conversed with Harry Rayner on the R/T. With Jim Wem as an observer, he then took off in Jet Provost XD694 at 1450 hrs, and as pre-arranged, the Jet Provost located the Gannet at about 4,000–5,000 ft locally. The Gannet's rear propeller was feathered and the Jet Provost flew underneath the Gannet where Frost attempted to release the Gannet's nosewheel with the airflow over the cockpit canopy. Despite several attempts, this proved unsuccessful and the Jet Provost returned to Bitteswell at 1539 hrs. It was decided to lay a foam carpet for the first 600 yards of Runway 22 and whilst this was in progress the Gannet remained at low level in the locality to use fuel. Eventually at 1620 hrs Harry made a perfect landing on the foam carpet with little damage to the aircraft and was flying again within weeks."

In March 1956, the Hunting sales team at Luton was joined by **G-AOHD**, which was allocated as a company demonstration aircraft to promote the Jet Provost in a variety of climates and conditions. Beginning in February 1957, test pilot Dick Wheldon flew the aircraft to the RSwAF Flying School at Ljungbyhed in Sweden, providing familiarisation flights for selected air force officers. The following month it was transferred to Helsinki to be demonstrated to the Finnish air force, where it spent a week, based at Malmi and Seutula; Capt Vilho Lukkarinen becoming the first of ten Finnish pilots to be given an experience flight in the Jet Provost before it returned to Luton.

The following April, the Jet Provost was shipped to Trinidad as part of an ambitious sales tour of nine South American countries during a four-month trip to Latin America. Flown by the company test pilot, Dicky Rumbelow, selected groups of pupils were also given ab-initio training to solo standard. The tour ended on 12 August 1958 when the aircraft was dismantled and shipped back to Luton.

During the tour, the Jet Provost had flown 8,400 miles during a total flying time of 178 hours, providing evaluation flights for 123 air force officers and visiting 27 airfields: Trinidad, Venezuela, Colombia, Ecuador, Peru, Chile, Argentina, Uruguay, and finally to Brazil in August, at which numerous demonstrations were given without any interruption to the flying programme.

By March 1959, the aircraft was shipped again to Australia to take part in a six-month trial with the Royal Australian Air Force to evaluate an 'all-through' jet-training programme. Issued with the serial, A99-001, the Jet Provost was operated by No. 35 Training Course at No. 1 BFTS, Point Cook, which began in May 1959 and included Flt Lt John Paule, a flying instructor who had previously converted to the aircraft at Bankstown, and two selected students Cadet Brian Morgan and Cadet C.V. Smith. Towards the end of the course, the aircraft suffered minor damage to the port undercarriage during a ground incident at Point Cook, which was subsequently repaired and the aircraft was returned to Bankstown in November 1959. At the conclusion of the evaluation, the RAAF decided not to order the Jet Provost as a basic-training aeroplane because of its limited role, and it was sold to the RAAF as an instructional airframe in May 1961. Following a period with Sydney Technical College it was placed into storage at the RAAF Museum, Point Cook, in 1985.

The third pre-production Mk 2, **G-23-1**, had been modified at Luton in early 1958 to become the prototype T Mk 3, but the cost of the development programme continued to rise due to the proposed installation of ejection seats and associated modification work. This included a complete redesign of the fuselage and canopy lines, rearrangement of the flying controls and stress testing of the airframe, all of which would require a significant increase on the initial estimates supplied by the company. Additional costs also encountered during the development trials –

ALL-THROUGH JET TRAINING IS HERE TO STAY

including the installation of UHF radio equipment and resolving the problems encountered with the undercarriage retraction system, which had been unique to the pre-production airframes – threw up more questions as to which department was responsible. In the end, the costs were borne out by a most reluctant HM Treasury.

In mid-1958, the aircraft was selected to take part in the Venom Replacement Evaluation Trial at Khormaksar, Aden, as the HQ, British Forces Arabian Peninsula had been able to persuade the Air Ministry to lay on a competitive evaluation project to find a new ground-attack aircraft to replace the RAF's Venoms operating in the Middle East. The evaluation would involve three contrasting aircraft types: the Hawker Hunter, the Folland Gnat lightweight fighter and the Jet Provost trainer. While the two CFE Hunters from West Raynham were flown direct from the UK, the Gnat and Jet Provost were flown out to Aden in a Beverley transport aircraft and re-assembled for the trials, which ran from 14–17 August 1958.

Operating from the airfields of Khormaksar and Riyan, the Jet Provost had been issued with a temporary military serial, **XN117**, and modified to carry machine guns and rocket and bomb carriers for the trial. Unfortunately, it was considered as a complete outsider from the beginning and, despite its low-operating costs,

Originally built as a pre-production T Mk2, G-23-1 was converted as the prototype T Mk 3. In 1958, it unsuccessfully took part in the Venom replacement trial in Aden as 'XN117', and was later evaluated in India and Pakistan. It was scrapped at Luton in 1962. (BAe Systems Heritage Warton-Percival/Hunting Collection)

The fourth and last pre-production Jet Provost T. Mk 2 G-AOUS flying with G-23-1. (BAe Systems Heritage Warton-Percival/Hunting Collection)

the Jet Provost failed to perform any of the operational tasks or firepower criteria to the required standard and was quickly eliminated. The Hunter eventually emerged as the clear winner of the trial.

From Aden, the aircraft was flown to India and Pakistan giving air experience flights and aerobatic demonstrations at seven different bases during the ten-week tour; the principal evaluations being made at Mauripur and Risalpur by the Pakistan air force and at Jodhpur by the Indian air force. **AM Pattathil Venugopal** was one of the Indian officers that watched the assessment.

"The first time I saw this aircraft was in 1958 when it was brought to No. 2 Air Force Academy/Air Force Flying College (Jodhpur) for demonstrations. From a trainer's point of view, it seemed very good; the spin and recovery at treetop height was lovely to watch and was also considered excellent for student pilot training. Two cadets Rajaram and Iqbal Singh were selected to fly with the company test pilot.

We were told Rajaram was fit to go solo after six hours and Iqbal Singh took about nine hours; they were not sent solo, however. Representatives of the flying and technical branches were there, and I think the station commander and CFI also flew the aircraft. The test pilot stayed in Umed Bhavan and Lofty Jatar kept him company with drinks and dinner. Our HAL Kiran was born not long after; it had some weaknesses and never came up to the standard of the Jet Provost."

The demonstration tour was completed in October 1958 and the aircraft returned to Luton, where it was placed into store and scrapped in early 1962.

The fourth and final Mk 2, **G-AOUS**, first flew in August 1956 and departed on a sales and demonstration tour of Canada and the USA, two months later. The RCAF wanted to replace its ageing Harvard aircraft with jet trainers and had demonstrated an interest in the Jet Provost following a visit to Luton by an evaluation team to examine and fly the aircraft. Together with the Jet Provost, a number of aircraft had also been selected for the evaluation, including the CM.170 Fouga Magister and the Canadair CT-114 Tutor.

In late September 1956, the Jet Provost was transferred to Kenting Aviation at Oshawa Airport, Ontario, the main flying base for Hunting's Canadian aerial survey subsidiary. From Oshawa, the Jet Provost was flown by chief test pilot Stan Oliver, who toured the RCAF bases at Ottawa and Trenton. However, despite completing a trouble-free schedule and flown by a number of service pilots, who spoke well of its handling characteristics, the RCAF eventually chose the Canadair CT-114 Tutor as its primary jet trainer. The Jet Provost then moved on to the USA, where it was inspected by representatives from the US Air Force and Navy in the Washington area before returning to the UK in October 1956.

By August 1958 it was fitted with the more powerful Viper ASV 11 and unofficially designated as the 'Jet Provost Mk 2B', and subsequently took part in the London to Paris Air Race in July 1959 and the SBAC show at Farnborough in September. A further sales trip to Portugal in October was slightly marred when it suffered a wheels-up landing at the end of the month while flown by Capitán (Capt) Oliveira Belo and Teniente (Lt) Braga Gonçalves at Sintra Air Base. Following repairs, it was later destroyed in a fatal crash at Langford Common, near Biggleswade in November 1959.

The respected aviation journalist, **John Fricker**, was provided with the opportunity to assess both the pre-production Mk 2, G-AOUS, at Luton and a T Mk 1 at Hullavington courtesy of instructor, Flt Lt Richard Tuffin:

Above: Ready to embark on the evaluation tour of Canada and the USA in September 1956. Clockwise from top: Ron J. W. Brown (salesman) standing on the wing, Stan Oliver (Hunting chief test pilot) in the cockpit, and Bill Kingwell. (BAe Systems Heritage Warton-Percival/Hunting Collection)

Below: Portuguese officers involved in the evaluation of G-AOUS at Sintra in 1958. Lt Conceigao, Capt Belo and 2nd Lt Braga Gonçalves. (via Diogo Eira)

"First impressions are likely to be particularly important, but the Jet Provost is so obviously a completely friendly little aircraft that its Spitfire-like performance is not likely to overawe the embryo pilot. Ground manoeuvrability is good, although in the Mk 1 on Hullavington's tarmac, I found the pneumatic braking system slightly too sensitive, and the long undercarriage tended to 'walk' disconcertingly with brake application; the short undercarriage and hydraulic Palmer toe brakes have completely cured the snags of the Mk 2. Pupils will feel completely at home in the Jet Provost, which is undoubtedly easier to fly than its piston predecessor."

Mention should also be made of **G-AOBU** which was included as an addition to the original contract for ten evaluation Jet Provost Mk 1s and was first flown in May 1955 for use as a company demonstrator and engine development aircraft by Hunting Percival Ltd, Luton, and Armstrong Siddeley at Bitteswell. Withdrawn in 1957, it was variously owned by the Shuttleworth Trust and Loughborough University until it was acquired by its current owner, Tim Manna of Kennet Aviation who repainted it as 'XD693/Q-Z' of No. 2 FTS in 1998. Following the termination of its Permit to Fly, the Jet Provost was placed into store at North Weald.

Stan Hodgkins had been a FAA observer before transferring to the RAF to begin pilot training at Leeming between 1966–1967. His subsequent association with a variety of aircraft included the Gnat, Hunter, Lightning, and Yorkshire UAS as a QFI. He then volunteered for SOAF, flying Strikemasters at Salalah during the latter days of the Dhofar War, followed by three years on the Buccaneer before leaving the service in 1980. After gaining a PLAT he joined a company at Cranfield training commercial pilots before going back to Oman to fly the Hunter for two years. Following his return to the UK, he undertook a variety of flying jobs but also flew ex-military jets on the air show scene, before going to Llanbedr to fly the Hawk and Canberra. This led him to join Martin-Baker as their company pilot flying the Gloster Meteor and Beechcraft King Air.

"In 1993 I was asked if I would like to fly a Folland Gnat which had been bought by an American owner. This turned out to be Tim Manna of Kennet Aviation at North Weald, who also acquired the Jet Provost T Mk 1 about that time from Loughborough University in 1991.

"Slowly the aircraft was restored by Pete Walker, Dave Horsfield and the team, and I was lucky enough to fly it at Cranfield for the first time since 1958, on 22 May 1994. After three further test flights we did the official CAA test flight on 8 June.

"Flying the JP1 was a rather strange experience. It was obvious at first sight that it had been cobbled from the earlier Provost at minimum cost. On first impression the tall undercarriage legs were puzzling. If they had taken the trouble to design a new retractable gear, why had they not shortened them? After all, there was no need for propeller clearance. The other feature was a miniscule jet pipe which hardly looked bigger than a hairdryer. The cockpit was also from an earlier era, with no bang seats and WWII instruments.

"We did several air displays and it attracted quite a lot of attention for a while due to its novelty I suppose. It had a curious quirk: the landing gear and flaps were operated pneumatically, and when we cycled the undercarriage during air shows sometimes only one leg would retract. Luckily three greens were always achieved before landing. An inverted flypast with one long leg sticking up was always a crowd pleaser.

"Performance was marginal and at the time engine problems were ongoing; on one flight the engine power started to steadily decrease and with the throttle wide open I just managed to get back on the ground from a glide approach with delayed deployment of the undercarriage and no flaps. On landing there was hardly enough power to taxi in. I think at that point the aircraft was grounded and modifications made to fit a later, more powerful version of the Viper."

EARLY CFS JET AEROBATIC TEAMS

With the conclusion of the jet training evaluation at Hullavington in November 1957, seven of the Jet Provost T Mk 1s, XD675-680 and XD693, were transferred to Central Flying School in Little Rissington to form an aerobatic flight. **Norman Giffin** arrived in April 1957 and was appointed leader of the team the following year:

"I believe the original idea of a Jet Provost aerobatic team came from AM Sir Richard 'Batchy' Atcherley, AOC Flying Training Command. Batchy was one the great characters in CFS folklore and had been a member of the school's aerobatic flight which participated at the popular Hendon displays between 1927 and 1930. He was very keen that we should try to introduce some inverted flying into our display routine and authorised the fitting of special inverted flight fuel systems to the aircraft. Unfortunately, the Jet Provost 1 was underpowered, which severely limited the formations that we could fly and also made any inverted display impractical.

"The team were all volunteers and included Flt Lts Don McClen, Fred Packer and Pete Millington, with Mike Edwards as the reserve. None of us had any previous

Jet Provost T Mk 1s that were part of the CFS Jet Aerobatic Team. (Don McClen)

experience of formation aerobatics. We wanted to call ourselves 'the Red Pelicans' but the previous Meteor team had aspirations to fly into the 1958 season and continue to use the name 'Pelicans'. In the end we settled for the rather uninspiring name – 'the CFS Jet Aerobatic Team'.

"Our first formation practice was on 3 March 1958 and we collected the team aircraft from St Athan on 2 April (I collected XD676) where they had been resprayed in the new red and white scheme (including XD675, XD676, XD678, XD679 and XD680) which I designed to emphasise the differences between the top and bottom surfaces. This was in anticipation of being able to do all or part of the routine, flying inverted, similar to that of the CFS Avro Tutor team in 1933. We made our debut at the RAFA display, Hucknall, on 26 May.

"In August 1957, it was also decided to fit some RAF Regiment battlefield smoke generators under each of the wings, operated by the landing light switch. They gave off a gratifying amount of smoke but on landing we found the wings under the fuel tanks were badly scorched and were eventually considered too dangerous."

Don McClen was also a member of the team. He had previously flown Meteors and Hunters with No. 257 Squadron, before qualifying as a QFI and appointed as a staff instructor at Little Rissington in July 1957:

"The turning point in my tour at CFS occurred with the arrival of five Jet Provost Mk 1 aircraft from RAF Hullavington in November 1957. I had my first flight on 2 December 1957 with Freddy Packer, a fellow instructor who had flown it at Hullavington. It was later decided that four of the aircraft should be assigned for a CFS formation aerobatic team.

"Volunteers were invited to apply for the team, and after several close formation flights to explore the performance and flying characteristics of our aircraft we discussed what sequences we should practise. It was agreed that Freddy Packer and I should investigate a pre-war CFS tradition of performing formation aerobatics with the aircraft connected by coloured streamers. So we attached a long piece of stout string to his cockpit, and fed the other end into my cockpit, allowing 20 feet of slack. Having agreed to test the limits in formation aerobatics while keeping the string from snapping, we took off in close formation. After a few tentative turns to allow us to gain confidence, Freddy tried some barrel rolls and loops. We quickly realised, however, that we would be severely constrained in the variety of manoeuvres we could perform if all of us were to be attached to each other in this way and concluded that there was no particular merit in further trials as the pre-war traditions were no longer appropriate – especially when the string snapped as we were landing and was ingested through my engine intake, causing the engine to fail.

"Our formation practices thereafter proceeded along more conventional lines and the team worked up to display standard over a period of ten weeks, in over 40 sorties. The display season took us around the country, and culminated in the SBAC show at Farnborough – 20 displays in all. Although we told ourselves that the cognoscenti appreciated our skills, our role was to entertain the general public. We were 'competing' that year with the Black Arrows which specialised in performing a loop of 22 Hunters. One day at the show, we had very severe turbulence and squally showers to contend with, and when flying inverted in the barrel roll, I was thrown out of position and my violent control movements resulted in my wingtip touching Norman's wingtip. Both wingtips had to be replaced and it had been a close shave.

"Endeavouring to cheer us up, Batchy, our staunchest supporter, snorted: 'Any self-respecting pilot can do a formation loop in a Hunter. But you are up against the stops for your entire display and I am proud of you!' Our spirits were also buoyed by a congratulatory letter from the designer of the jet engine, Air Cdre Sir Frank Whittle. A total of 17 displays were completed during the season, which was concluded with an appearance at RAF Cosford on 20 September."

The CFS Jet Aerobatic Team in 1958: Flt Lts Don McClen, Norman Giffin, Fred Packer and Pete Millington. (Norman Giffin)

A lack of available aircraft in 1959 led the CFS to provide two Jet Provost Mk 1s as a synchronised display pair – The Redskins. (Curly Hirst)

Subsequent correspondence between the commandant of the CFS and the senior air staff officer (SASO) regarding the possibility of forming a further Jet Provost display team in 1959 soon ran into problems: manpower shortages and difficulty with maintaining aircraft serviceability found the CFS unable to provide a display team of four aircraft for the new season. The lack of available aircraft was eventually resolved with the suggestion from SASO that it would be possible to divert two or three aircraft from the existing fleet of Jet Provost T Mk 1s (XD675–XD680) and work up a routine of synchronised aerobatics. Retaining the red and white colour scheme of the previous year's team, the Jet Provost pair became known as 'the Redskins', and comprised former Meteor night-fighter pilot, Flt Lt 'Jimmy' Rhind, together with seasoned display pilot, Flt Lt 'Curly' Hirst. Between May and October 1959, the team performed at 34 shows, the climax of which was the SBAC show in September.

The CFS Jet Provost T Mk 1s were also used for converting staff instructors and for the advanced phase of the student courses, with Flg Off John Goodwin of No. 191 Course becoming the first to complete his conversion training on the type on 19 April 1958. History was made once again on 15 April 1959, when Flg Off Ian Sheppard of No. 196 Course graduated as the first 'all-through' jet-trained pilot to complete an instructor's course at CFS without any previous piston-engined training. **Norman Giffin**:

"The syllabus for the Jet Provost Mk 1 was very similar to the one for the Piston Provost. There was a total of 18 exercises, of which the forced-landing practice was found to be much easier than in the Piston Provost. Although the original idea of jet training included high-level characteristics, the Jet Provost had no high-speed or high-altitude problems, except that it had a very slow rate of climb and just wasted a lot of time getting there. In many ways it was not as good a trainer as the Piston Provost as it was too easy to fly and I am sure quite a few students would have had problems when they went on to fly the Vampire T.11."

With the arrival of the first batch of Jet Provost T Mk 3s to the CFS, the T Mk 1s were withdrawn in November 1959 and issued to No. 27 MU Shawbury for eventual scrapping.

REGULAR SERVICE

In November 1957, No. 2 FTS and its establishment of 25 Provost trainers was transferred from RAF Hullavington to RAF Syerston. Two years later, the unit became the first to receive the Jet Provost T Mk 3, with flying training beginning in October 1959.

Fitted with ejection seats, wing tanks, and a slightly more powerful Bristol Siddeley Viper 102 engine, the first production Jet Provost Mk 3 (XM346) had made its maiden flight from Luton on 22 June 1958. Deliveries to the RAF began with an initial batch of ten pre-production aircraft being officially accepted by representatives from the Central Flying School and No. 2 FTS, Syerston during an informal ceremony at Luton Airport in June 1959.

From 1962 to 1989, **Reg Stock** was the Hunting/BAC project pilot for both the Jet Provost and Strikemaster. He had previously instructed on the Provost and Jet Provost at RAF Syerston from November 1958, and had also been a member of the school's aerobatic teams during this period:

"I had previously flown with the school's Provost display team as a member of a synchronised pair with Jock McTavish, and was later part of Syerston's first, short-lived, Jet Provost aerobatic team in 1960. My first flight in a Jet Provost Mk 3 (XM377) was on 22 January 1960 at Syerston and I completed a further 14 familiarisation/conversion flights – one of my first being a check ride (in XM403) with the flight commander, Sqn Ldr Keith Williamson, who later became Marshal of the RAF. By this time we had completed the last Piston Provost course and started our first Jet Provost course."

As it was accepted that not all units and foreign air forces had been equipped with jet aircraft, the school retained an establishment of Provosts to provide such training for another 12 months. Once the majority of the QFIs had completed their jet conversion training, the first all-through training course – No. 143 Course – began on 7 October 1959. A month later, on 9 November 1959, history was made again when **Acting Plt Off Olly Knight** became the first student to go solo on the Jet Provost Mk 3:

"In September 1959 I arrived at RAF Syerston in Nottinghamshire to begin training. We saw on arrival, a long line of orange-painted Provosts by the hangars; with others making their particular growl overhead in the circuit you can imagine the excitement felt by the members of No. 143 Course. Most of the rest were straight out of school but a handful of us were 'retreads' – previously signallers, navigators, teachers, doctors, equipment officers, and the like. The squadron, which contained two courses of student pilots, was at the time commanded by Sqn Ldr Keith Williamson (later CAS) and his first words to us were that these aeroplanes were not for us (cries of dismay!). No, we were to be the first Jet Provost Mk 3 course (cries of incredulity!). At the time there were many other basic flying training schools scheduled to be equipped with the Jet Provost and to be singled out as the first of the all-jet courses (I know there were earlier JP Mk 1 courses but they were more of a trial) was something very special.

"We quickly settled down to learn as much as we could as fast as we could. Days alternated between ground school and flights until we had passed all the ground tests. There were hurdles along the way of course and much of our circuit work was flown at the satellite airfield at Wymeswold, just off the Fosse Way north of Leicester.

"There seemed to be an inordinate rush to get me to solo standard and, dim as I was, I assumed that I needed extra coaching. My instructor, a lovely former Hunter pilot called Dai Jones, eventually declared me fit and, not for the first but certainly the most exciting time, off I went for one circuit and a landing in XM363.

"Careful pre-take-off checks, on to the runway, full power and away we went. Gear up, flaps up in the climb, roll onto the downwind leg, airbrakes, gear, flaps, fuel and harness and in we come for an arrival. Made it – and great applause from

ALL-THROUGH JET TRAINING IS HERE TO STAY

A depiction of members of No. 143 Course including Acting Plt Off Olly Knight. It was the only course not to have an official graduation photo. (Olly Knight)

Dai because I had pipped another student Geoff Denny by about three minutes to become the first student to go solo on the Jet Provost Mk 3; it is fair to say, however, that I had soloed in the Chipmunk at Henlow in March 1958 so Geoff was probably the first ab-initio student to make it in the JP Mk 3. The course was tough but greatly enjoyable, and after the navigation, low level, night-flying formation and instrument flying, it was time for the final tests and graduation before moving to the fast-jet training base at Oakington near Cambridge."

THE CFS LEADS THE PACK

In January 1960, the RAF's first Jet Provost Mk 3 display team was selected from the CFS at Little Rissington, which continued the school's enviable reputation for formation aerobatics when it began practising with four of the newly delivered aircraft as the Central Flying School Aerobatic Team. Former Canberra pilot and instructor at No. 1 FTS, **Ian Bashall** joined the CFS staff in January 1962. He was appointed as deputy leader of that year's aerobatic team and assumed the leadership of 'the Red Pelicans 1963', the following year:

"In 1962, the display team had been purely the CFS team. We had re-equipped with Jet Provost Mk 4s and had been nominated to appear at the Farnborough air show in September. After some persuasion by the commandant, we got Huntings to spray the aircraft all over with a subtle shade of red as we considered that the colour would have more impact with the public. It was also decided that the nine available aircraft would continue to operate with the smoke installations to enhance our display by replacing the second ejection seat with a drum of hydraulic fluid. I think our performance at Farnborough was well received and the only person we upset was Charles Gardner who was doing the commentary from the control tower.

Soon after receiving its Jet Provost Mk 3s, the CFS at Little Rissington formed the first display team to operate the type. From left to right: Gerry Nicklin, Roy Langstaff, Frank Brambley and Bruce McDonald. (BAe Systems Heritage Warton-Percival/Hunting Collection)

This was because we did a 'smoke on' formation landing and he was unable to see anything when it completely covered the tower. That part of our display was then banned for the rest of the week.

For the 1963 season there had been a change of policy, and we became the RAF team. We flew 33 shows that year, including the prestigious NATO display before 50,000 people at Lyon/Brice in France, which included contributions by teams from France, Italy and Belgium. We were presented with the Coup Shell Berre trophy for our fine display."

Tony Doyle was a staff instructor on the Vampire Flight at Little Rissington, transferring to Jet Provosts and as a reserve member of the station display team in 1962:

"The resident aerobatic team was still using the Jet Provost Mk 3 and they completed an overseas tour which went as far as Nigeria in October 1960. The Mk 3 was so underpowered that they were very limited in what they could do, and in January 1962 we started working up the Jet Provost Mk 4 team, Red Pelicans; with the extra power we could sport a five-ship and just manage rolls with five aircraft in echelon formation. There was always a section of the higher echelons who were ambivalent about display teams because they used a lot of resources and the risk of a 'scrunch' was high.

The Red Pelicans led by Flt Lt Ian McKee with the infamous one-off 'smoke on' landing at SBAC show at Farnborough in September 1962. (BAe Systems Heritage Warton-Percival/Hunting Collection)

> "I don't think the previous Mk 3 team had a 'mirror' formation in their repertoire, but the 1963 team led by Ian Bashall included that particular manoeuvre and during the work-up period the two 'mirror' aircraft touched fins; there was a dent in the top of the fin of both aircraft and tell-tale smears of paint. Ian, quite rightly, was looking for a way to keep this quiet, either because they had not yet been authorised or because it might 'spook' the management and get it prohibited. Ian went to inspect the damage with Mr Barber, the warrant officer who ran the support team. Ian said: 'I think we might have had a bird strike.' After a close look, Mr Barber responded: 'Yes sir. I think they might have hit a f****** Pelican.'"

At the end of the 1963 season, the Air Ministry announced that it was to withdraw the English Electric Lightning squadrons as representatives of Fighter Command's official display teams for operational reasons; faced with very little alternative as to a suitable replacement, it was eventually concluded that it would be more economical to appoint the Jet Provosts of the CFS Red Pelicans as the RAF's premier aerobatic team. It was also decided that it would retain the six aircraft line-up from the previous season, and to enhance the display two modifications were considered: the introduction of a changeable red/white/blue smoke system or a container mounted in the rear fuselage omitting 'multi-cracker' pyrotechnics. The latter idea was eventually dropped because of the safety aspect.

The team's first official display was at Little Rissington on 28 April 1964 for the Wright Jubilee Trophy event, followed by its public debut at North Weald on Whit Monday, 18 May. Two weeks later, the team made its first overseas appearance at Stavanger/Sola, Norway and, despite bad weather, it went through a series of formation changes, with each aircraft alternating red, white and blue smoke at various stages of the 12-minute routine. The low run in mirror formation by Flt Lt Herbert Lane, inverted above Flt Lt Brian Nice's aircraft, was also popular with the large crowd attending the event. With further shows in Belgium and France during the summer months, the team returned to Farnborough in September to take part in the SBAC show, giving a series of synchronised displays with the RAF's first team of Gnat aircraft from No. 4 FTS, RAF Valley, unofficially known as the Yellowjacks.

Terry Lloyd had previously instructed at RAF Syerston before he was posted to the CFS staff in June 1962. The following year he flew as No. 6 with the Red Pelicans and was appointed to lead the team in 1964:

"During the work-up for the 1964 formation aerobatic season we were practising a barrel roll in delta formation over Moreton-in-Marsh; three aircraft line-abreast with No. 4 and No. 5 sitting in the spaces between the front three aircraft. I entered the roll in a normal manner and as I rolled out, my No. 4 said that perhaps he had suffered a bird strike. I checked Nos. 2 and 3 who should have been on my left and right but found that my No. 2 was missing. A radio check showed that he was no longer with us and a visual inspection of the No. 4 aircraft (XR670) showed that his starboard wing tank was badly damaged. Having sent Nos. 2, 4 and 5 back to base, I checked the immediate area and located a crashed Jet Provost (XP639), which was on fire; a low pass also showed a lonely figure very close to the aircraft. I was delighted to see that Dick Fox had survived, having successfully ejected using the bottom seat handle, but had sustained back injuries and was unable to continue with the team. As a result Eric Tilsley joined us.

"The time allotted for the RAF participation at Farnborough was severely limited and it was decided that the Red Pelicans and the Gnat team from RAF Valley should

The highlight of the 1964 Farnborough show was the arrival of the mixed formation of the Red Pelicans and Yellowjacks Gnat aircraft for their impressive synchronised display routine. (Bristol Siddeley)

For the 1964 season, the Red Pelicans were nominated as the RAF's premier display team. From left to right: Flt Lts Eric Tilsley, Herbert Lane, Dennis Southern, Bill Langworthy, Brian Nice, Terry Lloyd and the team mascot 'Patrick'. (Terry Lloyd)

combine to represent the RAF in a display of aerobatics. We detached to RAF Valley in early August to enable this to be done. The differing performance and manoeuvrability had to be carefully considered: the Gnat used more height in both looping and rolling manoeuvres than the Jet Provost but with their higher speed the Gnats were able to spend less time in wingovers and repositioning. Initially the team leaders flew sorties to assess how to overcome the problems. As a result of trial and error it became obvious that it was essential that both teams commenced the display from a common datum point. Thus after individual formation take-offs by both teams a combined formation with the Gnats leading the Jet Provosts was decided upon. On arrival the two formations split and commenced the show with respective leaders varying the time and distance flown in wingovers to ensure that their teams were correctly positioned for each manoeuvre. With practice the teams were able to achieve a maximum of seven to ten seconds between consecutive display manoeuvres. Ideally the most impressive finale to the display would have been a pull-up by the Jet Provosts for a bomb-burst, with the Gnats pulling up through the stem of our smoke, followed by their split. Unfortunately this was not possible, as an allowance had to be made for the six Lightnings of 92 Squadron to fly through just prior to the ending of the coordinated display. Both teams therefore carried out their individual finale, which included our bomb-burst and a delta formation landing."

The Red Pelicans completed its scheduled programme of 25 displays at the RAF Biggin Hill and RAF Ternhill Battle of Britain 'At Home' events in September 1964. Although the team had established and maintained a successful image, it was realised that the Jet Provost was no longer a contemporary aircraft and that it was only the type of presentation and display flying that had enabled it to retain its popularity during the season. With the apparent success of the Yellowjacks' performance at Farnborough, it became obvious to many that the Gnat team from Valley would make an ideal successor to the Red Pelicans. Therefore, following the withdrawal of the Red Pelicans as the premier display team at the end of the season, the CFS found itself without an official Jet Provost team, having been replaced by the subsequent formation of the Red Arrows as the RAF aerobatic team in 1965.

CHAPTER TWO

THE JET PROVOST T MK 4 HIGHER AND FASTER

By early 1960, work at Luton had progressed on the Jet Provost T Mk 4 as a high-powered successor to the Mk 3 in response to a requirement for increased upper air work in the student's syllabus. The 40 per cent increase in power generated from the Viper 202 (ASV11) turbojet installed in the Mk 4 enabled it to attain speeds of 400 kts and climb to more than 30,000 feet in 15 minutes. Various design changes were made to the airframe to allow it to cope with the higher speeds from the increase in power, including slightly enlarged engine intakes and dorsal air ducts, together with a revised tailplane.

Two Jet Provost Mk 3 airframes, XN467 and XN468, were removed from the production line at Luton and modified to serve as prototypes for the T Mk 4, with the first aircraft (XN467) flown by the company chief test pilot, Stan Oliver on 15 July 1960. It was soon followed by the second prototype (XN468) in August which made its public debut in the flying display at that year's SBAC show at Farnborough.

Both prototypes subsequently joined the test and development programme at Luton, Boscombe Down and Filton, and quickly impressed the Air Ministry with their improved performance. An initial production order for 100 Jet Provost T Mk 4s to be built by Hunting Aircraft at Luton (the company being renamed the British Aircraft Corporation during January 1964) was signed, and between November 1961 and December 1962, a total of 185 Jet Provost T Mk 4s were eventually delivered to the RAF.

In March 1962, the CFS team became the first to operate the newly delivered Mk 4 and was named the Red Pelicans. (Ian Bashall)

In April 1962, No. 1 Flying Training School at Linton-on-Ouse took delivery of its first Mk 4, followed by No. 2 FTS at Syerston in May. Further units included Nos. 3, 6 and 7 Flying Training Schools, the Central Flying School, the RAF College at Cranwell, the College of Air Warfare (CAW) at Manby and the TWU at Brawdy.

The CFS at RAF Little Rissington received its first Jet Provost T Mk 4s, XP549 and XP550, in November 1961. **Tony Doyle** again:

"The introduction of the Jet Provost Mk 4 meant that more of the syllabus could be covered in the earlier stage of training, thus taking the pressure off the ageing Vampires, and I was transferred from the Vampire Flight to the Jet Provost Flight in 1961.

"The Jet Provost Mk 4s took over from the Vampire so the blokes on the first course had already done some basic work on the Mk 3. Instead of going to the Vampire Flight as previously they came to the new Mk 4 course and were destined for the 'new' advanced flying schools, equipped with the rather 'pansy' Jet Provost Mk 4 instead of the 'manly' Vampire and Meteor."

Roy Booth had been a member of the 'unofficial' CFS Jet Provost display team in 1965, equipped with the Mk 4 aircraft inherited from the previous year's Red Pelicans:

"I joined 209 QFI course at CFS in July 1961, and following graduation at the end of November 1961, I was posted to the recently established No. 3 FTS at Leeming. I returned to CFS (B Flight, 1 Squadron) in April 1964 and volunteered for the nascent Jet Provost team, led by Bill Langworthy. We were not allowed to call ourselves by the former, traditional CFS title, so 1965 was the only year that the Red Pelicans did not officially exist. On 13 April 1965 Dennis Southern bravely agreed to fly with me on my first formation aeros practice with Bill Langworthy, Dinger Bell and Cas Maynard. I owe all that subsequently transpired to Dennis's patience and nerves of steel.

"As an aside, during my OTU course at Kirton in Lindsey I became great friends with the student in the neighbouring bed, Dick 'Yarpy' Foster, who later became

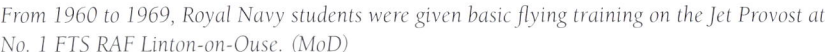

From 1960 to 1969, Royal Navy students were given basic flying training on the Jet Provost at No. 1 FTS RAF Linton-on-Ouse. (MoD)

the first student to solo in a Jet Provost in 1955. At the end of the course half of us (including me) were posted to Canada. Dick Foster went to Hullavington with the rest and ended up at Boscombe Down as a test pilot."

In 1966, Roy was selected as a team member to fly with the Red Arrows.

NO. 1 FTS LINTON-ON-OUSE AND NAVAL TRAINING

No. 1 FTS reformed at RAF Syerston in May 1955, equipped with Percival Provost T Mk 1s, and was responsible for basic flying training for Royal Navy and Royal Naval Volunteer Reserve students before they progressed to RAF Valley for advanced jet training.

In November 1957, the school moved to RAF Linton-on-Ouse and continued to provide initial flying training for all prospective Fleet Air Arm pilots, with the basic squadron flying Provosts and the advanced squadron equipped with Vampire T.11s. The naval students who graduated from Linton-on-Ouse were transferred to either RNAS Lossiemouth, Yeovilton or Culdrose for operational training.

Peter Hoar RN:

> "I was at Linton-on-Ouse with No. 77 RN Course from August 1958 to September 1959, flying the Provost and Vampire T.11. We had the first of two groups of Federal German navy officers – about six or seven on each of the two courses. I think the pass rate was as usual about 50 per cent."

Between August 1960 and April 1961, No. 1 FTS replaced its Provosts with Jet Provost Mk 3s and Mk 4s, which continued to operate alongside the Vampire trainers and became one of the last RAF Flying Training Command schools to operate courses for both types of aircraft: basic training on Jet Provosts and advanced training on the Vampires. Training began in October 1961 with No. 93 Course, a 'mixed' Provost/Jet Provost course. **VAdm Sir Jonathan Tod RN** was a member of No. 93 Course:

> "There were no previous students flying the Jet Provost but we did have Tom Cridland who was back-coursed from the Piston Provost as a result of a rugby injury, which

could have caused confusion leading to the idea that a 'mixed course' was being conducted. My first sortie in the Jet Provost was on 19 October 1960 and my last on 10 May 1961, before going on to the Vampire for advanced training and gaining my wings on 22 November 1961.

"On my first sortie of formation flying on 28 March 1961 the No. 2 had an engine fire and both pilots ejected; I was within feet of the incident and had an excellent view. Both crew members fired their seats in rapid succession and I have a clear memory of the vacant Jet Provost (XM477) gliding sedately with the two seat barrels sticking out above the cockpit. The student, Midshipman Mick Dugan, landed in a grassy field but this was occupied by a large grey horse who did not like trespassers; Mick had an aversion to horses and spent about ten minutes being chased by the horse – he later told us it was much more frightening than a mere ejection.

"The Jet Provost continued to fly for several minutes doing a gentle turn as if to join the circuit at Dishforth There was a long discussion as to whether one of us should close in on it to tip its wing causing it to crash before it reached the more populated area around York. Permission was not given. The aircraft finally crashed between Dishforth airfield and the A1 main road.

"We used to do our circuits-and-bumps at Rufforth airfield. On the date I can't remember but probably in the first fortnight of December 1960, a foreign

The Linton Gin team at RNAS Culdrose, 27 July 1963. (Tony Breese Collection)

student threw a 'wobbly' and could not land during his first solo. His instructor in the tower did a brilliant job in talking him down and then went to board the Jet Provost to fly it and the student back to Linton. Unfortunately in boarding the aircraft, whose engine was still running, he dropped his glove, which was ingested into the intake causing an engine fire. I don't think that the aircraft was a write-off.

"On 20 March 1961, Bill Langworthy took me on my very first two night sorties, which was my first preparation for night deck-landings on a pitching deck on various aircraft carriers when flying Buccaneers.

"I left Linton on 11 May 1961 and went to Lossiemouth, flying the Seahawk (a truly lovely aircraft) and the Vampire. Following my advanced training on the Hunter, I transferred to 736 Squadron in April 1962 to fly the Supermarine Scimitar – the 'E-Type' Jaguar of the skies – or was it 'The Beast'?"

With the gradual increase of Jet Provost T Mk 3s at Linton-on-Ouse, the station aerobatic team was reformed in February 1961 with a mix of RAF and navy instructors, comprising Flt Lt Ron Corck, Lt Carl Davis RN, Flt Lts Hugh Rigg and Dick Fox. Called 'Gin Section' the team gave its first display at RAF Dishforth on 10 June 1961; naval instructors would continue to be members of the successive station display teams until 1968, when Lt Dave Brittain RN became the last to fly as part of 'Linton Gin'.

Hugh Rigg explains the origins of the team's name:

"When I arrived at Linton in June 1960 the station aerobatic team comprised four Vampire trainers called 'Linton Blacks'. The Vampires were withdrawn in 1961 and it was during that year that the first Jet Provost team was formed, led by Ron Corck. It was called 'Gin Section' because Ron and I had both been on 60 Squadron in the Far East, in which the formations were not called the usual red, blue, green colours, but gin, whisky, brandy and vodka. We took over as the official station team and displayed at FAA Air Days and the RAF's Battle of Britain Days, together with the occasional ROC days."

Lt Chris Blower RN completed his National Service in the navy between 1954 and 1956, and ended up as a midshipman at 19 in command of a 71-foot motor torpedo boat converted for target work:

"I worked for Shell in the City, and remained in the RNVR then RNR spending weekends and the annual fortnight in minesweepers. I got a watchkeeping ticket, and was promoted to lieutenant RNR. However when I rejoined to fly in 1962, the Admiralty only let me start as a sub lieutenant, and I went to Linton soon after that.

"I trained at Linton on No. 103 course in 1962 flying the Jet Provost and the Vampire T.11. We started flying in early March 1962 with the JP3. The JP4s were introduced in June and were a great improvement, especially for high-level work because half the sortie in the JP3 was spent getting up to height. Out of 14 starters in 103 Course there were only five of us left on graduation, but many of those chopped went on to be successful observers.

"During my 15 months at Linton the students were all RN. The instructors were mixed however, about two-thirds RAF and one-third RN. My Jet Provost instructor was Flt Lt Chris Rowe, RAF."

With the impact of the government's latest defence cuts imposed upon the services, the arrangement for all basic training of naval fixed-wing pilots at Linton-on-Ouse came to an end on 31 July 1969 with the graduation of the last entry, comprising seven naval officers of No. 142 Course. These were replaced with training courses for both RAF and a small number of Commonwealth and foreign students, while the training of naval helicopter pilots with the EFTS was transferred to Church Fenton. The graduates of the final RN course at Linton-on-Ouse were: Lt R.J.B. Whiteway-Wilkinson RN, Lt N.V. Hayler RN, Lt A. Auld RN, Sub-Lt C.J. Williams RN, Sub-Lt K.P. Jones RN, Mid H.B.V. Reynoldson RN and Mid J.D.P. Worsley RN.

Richard 'Dick' King started with No. 4 Course at Linton-on-Ouse in December 1968:

"By then I had become senior student, and hence was the RAF student's parade commander on the final navy parade and also the same at my own wings parade on 17 October 1969.

"Back in those days the main runway at Linton was 22/04. On the far side of the airfield was the 'fire dump' and, to the best of my recollection, it contained three old aircraft which the Fire Section used for their practice drills. On the morning of the final RN parade, the early-morning airman who did the first airfield inspection was confronted by these three wrecks lined up on the main runway at the threshold

THE JET PROVOST T MK 4   HIGHER AND FASTER

point as though ready for a formation take-off. There was then a big panic to get them removed back to the dump because the VIP naval reviewing officer was due to fly in later before the parade.

"As an aside, our general service training officer was Sqn Ldr Bob Olding. He was an ex-navigator, and had won the DSC when on exchange with the navy onboard HMS *Eagle*. He was wounded in the legs by shrapnel whilst attacking Egyptian airfields during the Suez operation in November 1956. They crash-landed on the carrier with the wheels up and Olding lost his leg when it was amputated later in Cyprus. He was hence known as 'Clump'."

Stewart Lenton graduated at CFS as an instructor in 1966, flying both the Jet Provost Mks. 3 and 4. He was subsequently posted to RAF Linton-on-Ouse as a QFI in June 1967:

"Initially I was teaching FAA students on my only RN course, No. 133 (RN) Course, and I was allocated two students, of which Midshipman James unfortunately failed the course; the other graduated on 16 November 1967. My last flights with RN students were on 19 December 1967 with Sub-Lt Mick Blissett and Acting Sub-Lt Thomson on 28 December 1967. Mick Blissett was a 'natural' pilot and I gave him some pretty difficult exercises, which he coped with superbly. I understand that when he was later flying a Jet Provost the canopy blew off and he was left to land the aircraft in extremely difficult circumstances, with no radio communication possible. Mick went on to Harriers and played a major part in the Falklands campaign.

"My wife taught aviation medicine to the helicopter courses at Linton, as she was the unit medical officer there. I took her flying in the Jet Provost on several occasions; on one such she had gone up to Leuchars in the station Sea Prince, it went u/s for the return flight and I got permission to pick her up in a Jet Provost. I took all her flying kit but she asked, 'What about my flying boots?' I just told her to wear her shoes, but all she had was high-heeled stilettos. As she climbed into the cockpit, two Danish Hunters pulled alongside us and their eyes were out like organ stops on seeing this woman climbing in wearing stiletto shoes. Back at Linton she got some ribbing by the RN students, who reminded her about not wearing nylon (never mind nylons) when flying.

"When RN helicopter training moved to Church Fenton, a third Jet Provost squadron was formed on 9 October 1969 and I was the first flight commander until

Bob Turner took over a month later. My flight was the first in the RAF to use the Jet Provost 5 for instructional purposes."

The RAF's 50th anniversary celebrations at RAF Abingdon on 14 June 1968 was marked with more than 50 different types of RAF aircraft on show in one of its most comprehensive exhibitions before HM the Queen and the general public. The event began with a flypast of 31 Jet Provosts drawn from Linton-on-Ouse, Syerston, Leeming and Acklington, led by Wg Cdr L.A. Fergusson, OC Flying Wing, Syerston, which flew the Queen's cypher in formation over the Oxfordshire base: No. 1 FTS forming the 'E', 2 FTS and 3 FTS forming the 'II' and 6 FTS forming the 'R'. The official formation flypast was flown twice on 14 June; once for HM the Queen, followed by another for the general public.

Stewart Lenton was part of the No. 1 FTS contingent:

"In May 1968, we started training for the flypast. Initially the training was carried out at RAF Leeming with 38 aircraft, two of which were airborne spares. Then on 4 June we all flew down to RAF Gaydon which had just ceased being a V-bomber base. A member of the ground crew was in each aircraft. Here the runway was long enough for all 38 aircraft to line up together taking off in pairs at five-second intervals. I was near the back and my airspeed was reading the rotate speed of 75 knots before I released the brakes, due to the jet blast from the aircraft ahead. The take-off was extremely turbulent and I flew off the runway heading asap but gently as my No. 2 had to keep station on me. Being at the back of the tail end of the 'E' I had to have a safety pilot with me in case the 'E' closed up with the 'II'. The whole formation had six practices at RAF Gaydon and one initial one at RAF Abingdon.

"After the public flypast we flew in formation back to Linton with the call sign 'Sid's Mob': 1 to 12 in four Vic formations, close astern. That was all very well until on our return we started doing a few wingovers over Linton and a couple of the formation pilots had not been in the flypast so were not in such good formation practice. In such a tight formation there was no escape route and it got quite exciting. Though one might use another adjective."

David Jones had also been a member of the Jet Provost flypast over Odiham in 1968:

"I ended my tour at No. 6 FTS, Acklington, as part of the formation from RAF Gaydon in Worcestershire. We flew the royal cypher in honour of the Queen's attendance at the RAF's Golden Jubilee celebration at RAF Abingdon. Miraculously it was a success, and we flew it again at RAF Abingdon the next day, this time to please the crowds.

"The formation leader gave us meticulous briefings for the seven practices in June 1968 and the two actual flypasts and we returned to base on the 15th as 'Red Section'. So concluded a happy association with a delightful aeroplane."

NO. 3 FTS AND 'GEMINI PAIR'

No. 3 FTS reformed at Leeming on 15 September 1961, equipped with Jet Provost T Mk 3s. The first Jet Provost course consisted of 15 former UAS students, who had arrived on 4 October 1961 and began their flying training two weeks later. **Stewart Lenton** was on No. 2 Course at Leeming, from December 1961 to May 1962:

Pre-take-off checks by Plt Off Robin Renton of No. 2 Course, No. 3 FTS Leeming in April 1962. (Ken Parry)

"All of my course were ex-UAS, with at least 120 hours flying the Chipmunk, so we did 85 hours on the Jet Provost instead of the then customary 120 hours. We were the only Leeming course that trained solely with the Mk 3. There were a few Mk 4s there at the time, but not enough for all students to fly them."

On 3 April 1964, **Acting Sgt Plt Peter Gardiner** became one of the last non-commissioned pilots to graduate from RAF flying training and be awarded his wings:

"My father was a wing commander armament officer and was posted to Australia in 1956 for an exchange duty based in Melbourne. I finished school in Australia but ended up in 1958 with no UK school certificates. In January 1959 I took the entrance exam for RAF Halton Apprentice School and was accepted as an armament fitter u/t. I graduated from Halton in December 1961 and went to RAF Finningley on Vulcan bombers as an armourer. I later applied for aircrew training but did not have the required educational qualifications for a commission and was offered training as a sergeant pilot, which I accepted.

"I started with No. 8 Course, No. 3 FTS at Leeming in January 1963 with two other NCO pilots (Jim Lawn and Dave Cramp – the latter of whom became my best man when I got married the day after receiving my wings). I went on to fly choppers as NCO pilots could only be posted to either a Coastal Command or a helicopter squadron – Transport or Bomber Command would not take NCO pilots. At Leeming we flew both Jet Provost Mk 3 and Mk 4 aircraft and the course was a mix of commissioned and non-commissioned students, together with Rhodesian, Kuwaiti and Jordanian pilots. They were good chaps but one occasion that sticks in my memory was of a Kuwaiti/Jordanian student on a solo navex. He became uncertain of his position and called the Radar Unit for help. Asked, among other things, by the unit what his endurance was, he had difficulty in understanding the term and stated at the third attempt 'Sun Life of Canada'. In early 1963 I broke my nose playing rugby and was re-coursed with No. 9 Course and eventually graduated on 3 April 1964."

During the 1962 and 1963 display seasons, 3 FTS maintained a small number of Jet Provost aerobatic teams. In March 1968 however, the formation of the school's synchronised aerobatic team, 'the Gemini Pair' marked the first formal Jet Provost display team at Leeming for four years, and was in response to an official

The Gemini Pair team members Fg Off Ron Pattinson and Flt Lt Gordon Revell with the manager, Sqn Ldr Ernie Jones in 1969. (Ron Pattinson)

directive which called for a reduction in the number of four-ship display teams. Comprising Flt Lts Mike French and Euan Perreaux, the pair made its first public appearance at RAF Bentwaters in May and became best-known for the popular trademark 'mirror' formation manoeuvre in its display sequence.

By July 1970, the school had re-equipped with Jet Provost T Mk 5s, which prompted its paint shop to apply the logo 'the Gemini Pair' to the fins of five aircraft. **Ron Pattinson** was team leader of the Gemini Pair for both the 1970 and 1971 seasons:

"I arrived as a QFI at Leeming in March 1969 and began flying in the team with Gordon Revell, the following year. On 20 January 1971, whilst the team was working up for the new season, two Red Arrows' Gnats collided while performing the 'roulette' manoeuvre over Kemble, with tragic results. We had started our work for the season with no restraints at. That was at the end of February and the 'roulette' and 'scissors' routines were both still in our display sequence. It was only when someone picked up on a photograph in a local newspaper, which showed the 'roulette' during one of the displays, that the proverbial hit the fan and questions were asked about why we were flying the 'roulette' when the Red Arrows were not. We were then told to take it out of the sequence and to stop distributing publicity brochures showing the manoeuvre. This was in July and we had to revamp our routine completely."

Olly Knight was appointed as manager of the Gemini Pair in 1973:

"One of my flight commanders on No. 3 Squadron, 'Bob' Thompson, was the leader of the team and 'Dusty' Miller from No. 2 Squadron was the second pilot. We all had to do 'the day job' of basic instructing as well as practising and flying the displays and this usually meant an after-hours brief, a sortie and a debrief afterwards. The main feature of the display was the 'mirror' fly-by with one aircraft inverted and the other almost directly beneath it. We learned (and we were all new to the team) that we could space the aircraft laterally by a fair bit and it would look even more dangerous to the public on the ground – even though it was safer.

"We flew the Jet Provost Mk 5 at that time, a pressurised aircraft which made transits at high level (usually to continental Europe) much more pleasant although its navigation aids consisted only of a DME gauge. This proved to be a problem on one long-range transit. The Jet Provost with its straight wings and marked dihedral was very difficult to roll about its own axis and I spent a great deal of time sitting behind Bob in another aircraft and advising him while he mastered the technique of rolling inverted but maintaining the same flight path. He had John Galyer on board initially to show him the technique, but nevertheless it took time. We had to get this right before we could introduce other manoeuvres with both aircraft. At the same time we worked out a six-minute routine which showed the aircraft at its best. This comprised the famous Gemini inverted 'mirror' run, opposition manoeuvres (quite exciting to see the twinkling landing light approaching head on), barrel rolls, stall turns, loops, half-fleurs and so forth. Once we had perfected this at 5,000 feet we came down to 1,500 feet and finally to 500 feet as the display minimum. Finally the team had to demonstrate its ability at 500 ft to the AOC and this we duly did at Little Rissington in May at the same time as the Poachers from Cranwell, led by John Robinson, who was an old friend from my days at Church Fenton and Little Rissington some years earlier. We were then cleared to display both at home and abroad.

"One of the things I enjoyed most was the arrival home as a three-ship; we called this the 'T-Break' and comprised the team in line-abreast and me or Brian Fuller (the commentator) flying echelon on both. We would pull into a loop then break away in sequence from the inverted to land. I had no idea how much power was needed to fly over the top in this position. One had to put the throttle through the 'gate' to stay with it as we reached the upward vertical. No one ever complained about this manoeuvre in those halcyon days before the Hunter crash at Shoreham – and it was quite effective as an arrival.

"Having gained the head-shed approval we set off for Italy seven days later for our first 'proper' show at the Sia Marchetti factory airfield at Vergiate, to the north of Milan/Malpensa airport. In retrospect it might have been better to have given a few performances in the UK first, but that's how the cards fell. We took four aircraft so that the chief instructor, Wg Cdr Robin Blockey, could assess our professionalism. It also enabled us to take with us an MoD photographer, Pete Stevenson, in the hope that we could get some spectacular inverted-pair photographs over the Alps. On departure we flew over the station in 'box' formation – when there was suddenly an almighty bang from my aircraft. I thought we had hit the ATC tower or another aircraft but fortunately it was just that Pete had not properly locked the rudder bar and it shot down into the nose section as he put weight on to gain a better shot. The transit was a three-stage, four-hour flight via Manston to Dijon and finally to the Italian air force base at Cameri, from where we operated. The weather was not good over Europe for mid-May and our first excitement came on the handover from London Military to the French when a BEA Trident came out of a large cloud bank at the same height but in the opposite direction (we of course had no on board cloud/collision radar) – and passed through the spread-out formation. Not an auspicious start! We arrived in Dijon for a night stop, then set off in equally poor weather for Cameri. By this time we had run well out of navigation aids and were totally reliant on French and Italian radar units to get us to our destination. There was no hope of a Gemini inverted-pair photo shoot over the Alps as we battled our way in IMC at 30,000 ft, probably invading Switzerland in the process. The first we saw of Italy was from about 200 ft in 'box' formation about a mile from touchdown at Cameri.

"The Italians gave us a great welcome and whisked us away to the living accommodation off base. The team displayed the next day at Vergiate while I watched from the ground. It all went perfectly, in front of a large crowd of Milanese – a first success for Gemini 1973! The following day we flew a photo sortie over Lake Maggiore and Pete came home with some good shots. Just as well as, although the weather over the Alps was gin clear when we flew home, there was no way we were turning any aeroplane upside down with all those bottles of Italian plonk stowed in the cockpit. In all, this was a very enjoyable first show.

"Displays in Germany included Leipheim in Bavaria (memorable chiefly for a great sing-along afterwards in the mess with the 'Patrouille de France' team – and a FIAT G-91 pilot being sent home in disgrace after a very low but spectacular pass over the crowd). We used Wildenrath almost exclusively as a first point of call in Germany as the station was more used to handling all and sundry. The people at the various club airfields east of the Rhine always made us most welcome and I have warm feelings to this day for their hospitality.

We had one or two major frights and a few amusing moments too. It was at Krefeld that Bob performed one of his more alarming roll-outs from a barrel roll in marginal weather – and when No. 2 looked ahead again he was faced with 'the biggest and closest windmill I have ever seen'. Auf dem Dümpel also posed a challenge. We accepted the tasking but heard nothing from this civilian airfield before departure to Manston, Wildenrath and then Koln/Bonn airport from where we operated. They thought we were the same team as last year so sent us nothing. The team borrowed a map from the Arrows who were also performing there, got the RT frequencies for the display and set off, first to have a good look at the display area and line and subsequently to fly the display. On return to Kleine-Brogel, Bob told me that the display had gone well and there were no concerns. On return home I got a call from the AOC. The C-in-C RAFG and COM2ATAF, Sir Christopher Foxley-Norris had been at the show in his capacity as honorary vice president and had not been impressed by the team repeatedly overflying the VIP tent in which he sat. This was apparently some distance from the 'crowd line' and Bob had rightly ignored it. I had to put on my No. 1 uniform and report to Brampton forthwith. I explained the lack of communication from the local aero club and never once pointed out that the C-in-C might not wish to be so closely associated with a cavalier organisation, although I did say they were lucky to get a display at all. We heard no more about it. All told this was a very enjoyable time for us all and I think the experience made us better pilots too. Bob went on to lead other aerobatic teams within and outside the air force, while Dusty flew Jaguars and is now a retired air marshal and knight of the realm."

Due to the impact of the fuel crisis, 1973 became the final year for the majority of RAF display teams for reasons of economy and the Gemini Pair was disbanded, having made its last appearance at Duxford on 14 October 1972.

THE COLLEGE OF AIR WARFARE/ SCHOOL OF REFRESHER FLYING AT MANBY

The College of Air Warfare/School of Refresher Flying at Manby was among the last flying training units to equip with the Jet Provost Mk 4, which gradually replaced its Gloster Meteors during February 1964. The following year it produced the station's first Jet Provost display team and made its debut at Elstree on Whit Sunday, 5 June 1965, led by Flt Lt Bill Shrubsole.

Alan Sheppard joined the School of Refresher Flying in December 1964 and flew with the display team between 1965 and 1967:

> "The team started off as the RAF College of Air Warfare Formation Aerobatic Team and retained this title for at least the first three years. Various names for the team had earlier been mooted, including 'Astrals' and 'Magistrates'; these had been coined

Members of the Macaws display team. From left to right: Flt Lts Bill Shrubsole, John Wingfield, Ricky Stalker and Jim Adams. (Bill Shrubsole)

by Terry Bliss and were only crew room banter and *never* used. We only did seven displays the first year, but things later picked up as Flt Lt Bill Shrubsole's leadership strategy paid off and our reputation grew. Bill later revised the team's presentation and named it as the Macaws in readiness for the 1968 season."

Flt Lt Brian Hoskins arrived at Manby in May 1969 and subsequently flew as No. 3 with the 1970 display team. The following year he was appointed as the leader of the Macaws, which made its debut at Mildenhall on 22 May and subsequently performed at a further 16 shows in the UK, Belgium, France, Italy and the Netherlands. The highlight of the year was undoubtedly its appearance at the major international air show at the Aviano Air Base in June, when it displayed alongside teams from Italy, Belgium, France and the USAF.

"I failed my original basic flying test at Leeming and was told that I would never be a fighter or aerobatic pilot. After passing my second basic handling test, I really 'took off' and was close to the top of the course for flying. I went to Valley and really loved flying the Gnat and after Hunter conversion went to Singapore on No. 20 Squadron. The Red Arrows were formed whilst I was training and were well established when I returned to the UK in 1968. I went to CFS and wanted to instruct on the Gnat but there were very few slots available to my course.

As the team lacked the navigational aids to fly in busy airways, the Macaws followed a HS Dominie to and from Aviano in Italy for an air display in June 1971. (Brian Hoskins)

"From 25 June to 29 June 1971 we followed a Dominie navigation trainer to and from Aviano in northern Italy for the air display. It developed into quite a story and I am not sure why we were tasked to do it but I think it was because the Red Arrows were not available; possibly in the USA. It was a long way for a Jet Provost team to travel for one 20-minute display. The aircraft did not have the navigational aids required to fly busy airways, and in case the weather was bad over the Alps it was decided that we should fly in formation with a Dominie from Strubby. We got there after refuelling at Évreux, Dijon, and Turin – total flying time of four hours and 30 minutes.

"Most of the international teams and our display were well received. At the end of the flying display the Thunderbirds display team was amused to find us turning round and refuelling our aircraft – we did not have any engineers with us. They were even more surprised to meet us at the reception in the same flying suits.

"The next day was Sunday and we were going to Venice for the day. Just before we left the hotel I was told that they could not replenish our oxygen tanks. It seems that despite assuring us that they had all the NATO fittings, they did not have one for our system. They said that the Italian engineers planned to cut our pipes and fit a new connector. I said that they should not touch our aircraft and I asked them to continue their search for the NATO fitting.

"At the airfield the next day they had not found a fitting but felt sure that there would be one at the FIAT factory at Turin airport. If the weather over the Alps had been good we could have found a way through without flying above 10,000 feet, but it was dreadful. We flew to Turin but found the factory closed for a bank holiday. By now Training Command was involved and they told us to fly to Nice where BEA could probably help us. If not, we could go on to Istres. We flew low level to Nice along a sun-drenched coast and thousands of people on the beaches and at the airport. After landing the team members hoped that we might have to stay the night in Nice; I left them saying that we would have to go on to Istres. I went to the BEA maintenance building to be told that they could not help us but pointed at a notice for me saying 'under no circumstances were we to fly to Istres today and do not arrive there until after 1030 tomorrow'. Until now, the Dominie had followed us from Aviano but the next day they went back to base whilst we went to Istres for oxygen/fuel. We then flew home via Dijon and total flying time from Aviano was six hours and 40 minutes. Much easier than when I took the Red Arrows there in 1980 – one hour and 50 minutes direct.

The presentation of an award to the team at the international air show at Aviano in June 1971. The team included Dave Brooke, Brian Hoskins, Martin Engwell and Pete Diggance. (Brian Hoskins)

"On reflection, I was only 27 and leading one of the RAF's amateur aerobatic teams. I am not complaining because it was a wonderful experience for a young officer and prepared me for leading the Red Arrows eight years later. After Farnborough, Paris and RIAT, the Aviano Air Show was probably the biggest in Europe; it was more like RIAT than the other two which are industry orientated."

In December 1972, Brian left the CAW and eventually became a member of the Red Arrows aerobatic team in September 1974, which he led some five years later.

NAVAL TRAINING (CONTINUED)

Although the basic training of naval fixed-wing students at Linton-on-Ouse had been completed in July 1969, the training for those destined for a rotary flying career was transferred to the Royal Navy Elementary Flying Training Squadron (EFTS) at RAF Church Fenton. The EFTS was eventually returned to the aegis of No. 1 FTS in 1984.

In May 1976, the decision by the Royal Navy to order the Sea Harrier FRS.1 and to revive the training courses for suitable pilots to equip the future squadrons was made. The majority of the naval graduates at the EFTS had been posted to RNAS Culdrose to fly helicopters, but those selected for the prospective Sea Harrier squadrons were transferred to Linton-on-Ouse for basic training on the Jet Provost. In July 1976, the first three naval fixed-wing students – Lts Bill Covington, Greg Browne and Hugh Slade – joined No. 13A Jet Provost course and graduated in January 1977; the reviewing officer at the parade was RAdm John Roberts, Flag Officer Naval Air Command. Lts Slade and Covington later flew Sea Harriers with 809 Squadron during the Falklands War.

Cdre Bill Covington RN was one of the three naval students on 13A course:

"The course was a bit of an early hybrid, as the Sea Harrier student pipeline proper started one or two years after us. We joined the RAF students on the basic course at RAF Linton, they were 13 Course, and the three of us ran alongside them as 13A Course. However, because the RN was chasing a deadline for us to get to the Fairey Gannet in January 1978, we had to get through the basic course on the JP3A and the fast-jet lead-in course on the JP5 between May 1976 to January 1978.

"The RAF did us proud, giving us priority whenever they could and the basic course was abbreviated to some extent because we had already completed the 75-hour RN elementary flying training on the Scottish Aviation Bulldog. The RNEFTS and the RAF basic flying training course were very similar in content: a basic jet with a retractable undercarriage rather than the piston-powered Bulldog. My first solo was conducted at the relief landing ground at RAF Rufforth. I completed 70 hours 40 minutes on the JP3 course between 27 May and the final handling test on 27 August. I also see I regularly flew two or three times a day to average about 23 hours a month. It was superb.

"The fast-jet lead-in course on the JP5 was a delight. Suddenly we were in an aircraft that was air conditioned and pressurised, with the power to climb to height fairly quickly for upper air work, and could do 300 kt low-level navigation. This four-month course gave me 57 hours 15 minutes, with a focus on formation lead, more solo time with 18 hours 35 minutes and 32 hours 45 dual, plus two hours 45 minutes solo night and three hours ten minutes dual night. Nine hours was on instruments.

"As I said, No. 4 Squadron at RAF Linton could not have treated us better, we were a novelty and I would say they enjoyed having a more mature threesome of naval students. We were all general list, Hugh Slade and I were seaman specialist so we had completed three years at Dartmouth including a year as midshipmen in the Fleet, whilst Hugh had done two short jobs at sea (including one on the Royal Yacht) and I had done one sea job as a navigator. Greg Browne was an air engineer so had been through the RNEC at Manadon.

"The reason for all this was the procurement plans for the Sea Harrier FRS.1. The RN had realised that while the ex-Phantom and Buccaneer pilots would fill the senior jobs in the first SHAR squadrons and the new training pipeline would deliver the junior 'Joes', there would be a gap in mid-seniority lieutenants to fill the staff officer type jobs. So the three of us were pulled back from our basic helicopter course at RNAS Culdrose and sent to RAF Linton to be accelerated through to 849 NAS at Lossiemouth to fly the Gannet for two years, between 1977–78. This gave us carrier experience on HMS *Ark Royal,* before we started the fast-jet training in 1979, finally converting to the Sea Harrier in 1980.

"In some ways 13A Course was the beginning of the new era, but the first proper pipeline course started a year or two later than us with Lts Andrew McHarg and Mike Hale on it. There were also more hybrid conversions going on through Jet Provost courses for the RN helicopter pilots who were recommended for fighter jet conversion.

"As you can imagine the appointers were trying to fill the Sea Harrier squadrons with a mix of experience and above all fill the positions of the seven pilots required in 800/801 Squadrons NAS. It was an exciting time, and led into the Falklands in 1982, when all that effort to get Sea Harrier pilots trained paid off."

Hugh Slade was the third member of No. 13A Course:

"I went to Linton as a lieutenant in May 1976 along with Lts Bill Covington and Greg Browne. I first flew the Mk 3A on 27 May 1976 and went solo on 8 June. All three of us had completed the RNEFTS course on the Bulldog at RAF Leeming and recently started the helicopter BFT on the Gazelle at Culdrose when we were taken off it and sent for fixed-wing training – approval for the Sea Harrier had recently come through and my recollection is that we were the first naval pilots to go for fixed-wing training for quite a long time. The navy was keen to get us back asap and our course was conducted at a pretty brisk pace.

"We went on to fly the JP5 at Linton and on completion went to Lossiemouth to fly the Gannet AEW 3, in which we all did an embarked stint in HMS *Ark Royal.* Their lordships were keen to get us some deck experience and had we gone through AFT and TWU, followed by the Phantom or Buccaneer OCU, the *Ark Royal* would have been no longer – hence the Gannet. My first trip in a Gannet of 'B' Flight 849 Squadron at Lossiemouth was on 26 January 1977. After about two years on the Gannet Covington and I rejoined the RAF training pipeline (Valley, Brawdy, Wittering) en route to the SHAR. Browne was an air engineer and went back to doing engineering stuff.

Gp Capt Paul McDonald had been CI and OC Flying Wing at Linton-on-Ouse as the training of naval fixed-wing students on the Jet Provost was being gradually phased out in 1992:

"The RN had always been an important feature of life at Linton, and whatever criteria had been used to select Fleet Air Arm pilots, it was spot on. Their students were invariably charismatic and keen, all very much individuals, but totally focused on the need for naval aviation and the route that they had chosen. By 1992, the RN staff and students made up almost a third of No. 1 FTS.

"The last two RN students I flew with on the Jet Provost were Lt Lindsay on 1 October 1992, and Lt Wood on 23 November 1992. The sortie with Lt Lindsay was the Student Aeros Competition so he had obviously successfully completed the course by then and would probably have graduated the same month. The sortie with Lt Wood was low-level introduction so he would still have had some way to go. He could have been on the last Jet Provost course, but I can't say that for sure. Courses were about two months apart. It was rare for there to be more than one RN student per course, occasionally two, often none."

CHAPTER THREE

JET PROVOST MK 5
THE MG SPORTS CAR OF THE SKIES

Previously, the RAF's Jet Provost Mk 3s had been operated to teach basic handling procedures at the training schools before the student progressed to the Mk 4 for more applied instruction. This phase of the syllabus included aerobatic and high-altitude training sorties of up to 35,000 feet, which made great demands on the fatigue life of the Mk 4 wing and was a factor that would eventually lead to the withdrawal of most of the type from the service by 1971.

The requirement for increased high-altitude work also led to the aircrew being affected by decompression sickness – a painful condition in the muscles and

Jet Provost XS231 (H.166) first flew in March 1965 and was a flight test bed for the Viper 20 engine and a performance model for the T Mk 5. (BAe Systems Heritage Warton-Percival/Hunting Collection)

joints. The company response to the problem was the Jet Provost Mk 5 which, although a development of the previous Mk 4, was considered a completely new aircraft, with significant design changes which distinguished it from the earlier Jet Provosts. These included a lengthened and streamlined front fuselage nose incorporating a pressurised cabin, air-conditioning system, redesigned windscreen and two ejection seats. Also fitted was the Viper engine of its predecessor and re-designed 'export' wings with a greater fatigue life; the latter being fitted with hard points, capable of the possible carriage of external fuel tanks or underwing stores and a fuel capacity which reduced the requirement for tip tanks.

Most of the work for the new project had been completed at Luton, with two prototypes being converted from production T Mk 4s in 1965. In parallel with the Viper 11/BAC.145 programme, the second prototype, XS231, was modified for flight evaluation purposes of the Viper 20 engine and designated H.166. It first flew at Luton in 1965. **Dave Croser** was a flight test observer with Hunting and BAC:

> "It was in March 1965 that a numerically out-of-sequence Jet Provost (XS231) was allocated for flight testing with a Viper 20 engine, as the performance model of the proposed Jet Provost T Mk 5. It was in fact a Mk 4 airframe with increased power, and distinguished for company identity as the Hunting H.166. This first flight took place on 16 March 1965, flown by 'Dizzy' Addicott, with myself as the observer. The inherent increased power was immediately apparent on performance, together with the fact that it was a hybrid aircraft, which impacted on the aircraft's handling."

With the transfer of Jet Provost work to the British Aircraft Corporation factory at Warton in 1966, further construction was delayed, with the first prototype, XS230 – officially designated as a T Mk 5 (Interim) – making its initial 30-minute test flight by Reg Stock on 28 February 1967.

The changed airflow of the new nose section altered the handling characteristics to such an extent that a flight test programme was required to re-examine the stalling and spinning characteristics of the aircraft. To this end, in April 1967 the first prototype was evaluated at Boscombe Down, where the stalling, lateral and directional characteristics at high Mach and the spinning behaviour were found to be unsatisfactory for a basic flying training aircraft. A subsequent period of intensive flight testing by BAC with the two prototype aircraft occurred to improve the handling characteristics of the aircraft, after which the following modifications were recommended for embodiment: two small slats fitted to the leading edge of each wing root to improve the stall behaviour, while nose strakes would correct the unacceptable oscillations during the spin and also act as spoilers to reduce body damping. To minimise the effect of any wing inconsistencies at a high angle of attack, the outer-wing leading edges were roughened with a two-part paste called 'Camrex', and to improve directional damping a small plate was fitted to the fuselage below the rudder

In July 1968, a one-off contract for 110 Jet Provost T Mk 5s was signed and deliveries to the CFS, Little Rissington, began in September the following year. **Sqn Ldr John Robinson** was the OC Standards Flight at CFS during this period:

"I was tasked with the introduction of the Jet Provost T Mk 5 to Training Command. On 19 September 1969 I carried out the acceptance air test on Jet Provost T Mk 5, XW287, with Flt Lt Alan Elsegood of the Examining Wing. This was the first Jet Provost T Mk 5 to come to us and we flew over 18 hours on this aircraft while carrying out the trials to establish the differences in handling techniques and formulating procedures compared to the Jet Provost T Mk 4. The JP5 was based on the BAC 167 Strikemaster that was being built for export. It was a cleaned-up version of the JP4 and used the same engine although the Strikemaster had a more powerful one. It had extra internal fuel so the tip tanks were not necessary, which proved to be a great help with formation flying. The aircraft was partially pressurised so high altitudes could be attained which led to it being heavier than the JP4 but with the cleaned-up airframe performed just as well. All-in-all it was quite an improvement on its predecessors.

"As with any new aircraft on a unit everyone wanted to try it out and several trips were flown checking out the hierarchy of the station and then the staff QFIs. I also had to visit other units checking their Standards Flight pilots out as the JP5s were arriving quite frequently from BAC at Warton. There was a spate of engine compressor stalling problems and several air tests were flown to resolve the problem. I did have one that flamed out in a loop at 35,000 feet overhead Pershore, just north of Little Rissington. I transmitted a Mayday call on the Little Rissington approach frequency and was rather taken aback by the response to 'Standby'! Fortunately the engine relit without any further problem. Some units flying the JP5 reported issues with spinning the aircraft and I was sent to sort these out. I soon discovered what the cause was that pilots were applying full-spin entry control at speeds in excess of 15 knots above the stalling speed causing the aircraft to tumble rather than enter a spin, not a good technique. On 14 October I carried out the acceptance air test on a further aircraft, XW288. Subsequently other Jet Provost T Mk 5s were added to the fleet and conversion flights were carried out on the Jet Provost instructors. In December 1969 I had a hand in training the Red Pelicans pilots for the 1970 season, who were to form the team on the Jet Provost T Mk 5. Subsequently I had to convert the CFS instructors to the type and assist with converting pilots at other flying training units."

The 1970 CFS display team became the first to operate the new Mk 5 aircraft, led by **Sqn Ldr Eric Evers**:

"I had previously flown the Jet Provost Mk 4 with the 3 FTS display teams during the 1963 and 1964 seasons. Following my appointment as deputy CFI at Little Rissington, I first flew the Jet Provost 5 (XW287) on an 'evaluation' sortie on 15 October 1969. My own view was that the Mk 5 was certainly better for formation aerobatics than the earlier marks because of the cleaner airframe and lack of tip tanks.

"Our first public display was at Blackbushe airfield on 25 May 1970. The team aircraft were not fitted with smoke-making equipment and we subsequently flew 23 displays that year. One show in particular stands out in my memory, not for the display but for some hairy moments on the return journey. The display was at Regensburg in Bavaria and was very well received by the large crowd, helped by the fact that we were the only display team in the whole show. Later that evening we were entertained at a very enjoyable party with lots of Bavarian beer and 'oompah' music.

"The next day we started on the first leg of our return journey to Wildenrath in a loose formation against a prevailing westerly wind, low cloud base and a tight fuel state. The radar-controlled descent to the airfield, in cloud, went as planned. Now it's at this point, as any experienced aviator will tell you that 'Sod's Law' usually takes over and destroys your complacency in a flash, sure enough it did. 'Red Leader Radar unidentified aircraft ahead crossing you left to right, same height – turn right immediately!' The economy with words and the urgency in his voice spoke volumes and stopped any idea I might have of continuing the discussion. 'Pelicans turning right – GO' was my immediate response. I suddenly felt as vulnerable as the lead duck in a flock just about to fly over the guns of the local shoot as this unguided missile of an aircraft headed towards us in cloud giving him a target the size of a football pitch to aim at. The next few seconds seemed like an eternity but thankfully the danger passed without incident and slowly we came around again and landed exactly as planned. The rest of the return journey went as planned but that approach and landing at Wildenrath remains as clear as if it was yesterday."

An Australian exchange pilot who flew with the CFS, **Flt Lt Bruce Byron** was selected as a member of the Red Pelicans in 1973. He later went on to command RAAF CFS flying Aermacchi MB-326s between 1982 and 1983 and also selected/supervised the Roulettes display team:

"The 1973 CFS team consisted of two other exchange officers, Lt Marcus Edwards RN and Capt Dick Lord USAF, and was led by Sqn Ldr Ivor Gibbs RAF – a truly 'international' team. Our black flying suits were standard ones dyed black and had been used by previous Red Pelicans. The red suits we wore most of the time were sourced through a company that made F1 motor-racing suits [Jays racewear] by Ivor Gibbs and Adrian Wall. I still have mine.

"We had no idea it was the last Pelican year. From memory, the oil crisis hit after we had finished our display season, and as a consequence in early 1974, the decision was taken not to have another team. I was still there as one of two Jet Provost Standards instructors until June 1974 and I recall the restrictions on flying hours. However, planned courses all went on as usual. Little Rissington closed in 1976 so there was no impetus to get the Pelicans up and running again after the CFS moved to Cranwell.

"Another point of interest with the Red Pelicans 1973 was the number of displays we did. Normally the Pelicans did about 30 displays in a season, since Monday to Friday all pilots had flight instruction duties. In 1973 we did 51 displays, including seven on the continent, thanks to the drive of the leader, Ivor Gibbs – assisted by the manager, Adrian Wall. In the same year the Red Arrows did 100 displays – and that was their full-time job."

NO. 1 FTS RAF LINTON-ON-OUSE

In December 1969, No. 1 FTS at Linton-on-Ouse became the first training school to receive the new Jet Provost Mk 5. **Sqn Ldr John Robinson** again:

Jet Provost T Mk 5A, XW299, had originally been operated by No. 1 FTS at Linton-on-Ouse before being relegated as an instructional airframe at Halton and Cosford. Purchased by Jet Art Aviation in January 2013, it later went to Boscombe Down Apprentice School before being exported to Australia as G-CLJW in October 2019. (Jet Art Aviation)

"I spent a day at Linton with conversion flying for David Coldicutt and Sqn Ldr John Wheeler, who was the OC Standards Flight at Linton. I flew XW289 from Little Rissington to Linton early in the day on 5 November 1969 with Fred Lundy, one of my Training Flight instructors; it was a CFS aircraft so the conversions were in anticipation of the arrival of the Jet Provost 5 at Linton."

David Coldicutt had been a member of the Standards Flight at Linton-on-Ouse and had also flown with the station's display teams in 1969 and 1970:

"No. 3 Squadron at Linton was the first to get the JP5 with the arrival of two aircraft, XW298 and XW299, at the end of December 1969. I carried out a couple of conversions of the station QFIs when our aircraft arrived, and I see that I flew a couple of solo student conversion training flights in XW298 between 8–12 January 1970, and then an air test on XW296 and a conversion ride with Sqn Ldr Bob Turner on 22 January. I then flew a conversion ride with Flt Lt Jim Hunter, who was also in Standards on 25 January, so those two would have been among the very earliest to be converted. The Blades station display team started training on 31 January and I flew XW301 on that day. But it wasn't until I returned to No. 1 Squadron as 'A' Flight commander in June 1970 that I started instructing on the JP5."

Fg Off Steve Carr became the first student to receive instruction on the Jet Provost Mk 5 at Linton-on-Ouse:

"I was on No. 8 Course, from September 1969 until September 1970. My first jet flight was in Jet Provost Mk 3, XM472, on 13 October 1969 with Flt Lt Marchant. My first jet solo was in Jet Provost Mk 3, XN508, at Elvington airfield on 30 October, launched off by Flt Lt Alick Nicholson, who, as was the norm then, remained my main instructor throughout the whole year of the basic flying training course. The next six months consisted of re-enforcing all the special handling techniques required when things go wrong. Sorties would include a normal departure, perhaps a navex and/or aerobatics but invariably conclude with a simulated engine failure or fire, a hydraulic/electrical/undercarriage/flap/throttle failure. The emphasis was on knowing the published drills by heart, but at the same time recognising the specific unique aspects of each event and managing them intelligently. Then, on 18 March 1970, I became the first student to fly the new Jet Provost Mk 5 (XW297) with my instructor, Flt Lt Tim Allen."

Barry Hobkirk was also a member of No. 8 Course at Linton:

"I completed my first Mk 5 solo on 4 May 1970 after three hours and five minutes dual training. There were also three Jordanian students on our course, one of which Lt Talib al Zuarbi was lucky to escape a deep stall on finals during a practice glide approach during March 1970. He impacted the sports field at Linton right in front of me with such force his 'bang seat' broke free and fired the canopy but was millimetres from firing the seat. Lucky for him as the JP Mk 3 seat was way outside its operating range. One of the flaps from his cab was put on the wall in the 3 Squadron crew room, signed by us all."

Tim Allen had qualified as an instructor at CFS in September 1968 and was subsequently posted to No. 1 FTS, where he became the solo/reserve pilot for the station display team during 1969. He remained at Linton-on-Ouse until June 1970, when he was transferred to the Pakistan Air Force Academy. Returning to the UK, he graduated as a test pilot at Boscombe Down in 1980:

JET PROVOST MK 5   THE MG SPORTS CAR OF THE SKIES

No. 8 Course was the first course to graduate on the Jet Provost Mk 5 at No. 1 FTS Linton-on-Ouse in September 1970. (Barry Hobkirk)

"My previous experience of aircraft when I got to Linton was that I thought that the Jet Provost, with manual controls, was a very modern aircraft and I enjoyed flying it. I first flew the Mk 5 (XW296) with my boss, Sqn Ldr Bob Turner (OC No. 3 Squadron), on 27 January 1970, and carried out my first student sortie on 18 March 1970, with Fg Off Steve Carr in XW297.

"I loved aerobatics and had won several previous competitions at UAS on the Chipmunk, the Jet Provost at Leeming, the Gnat at Valley, and became the solo aerobatic display pilot for Linton in 1970 with the Mk 5. I did not have a special aircraft, just flew whatever was available, and made my first public display at RAF Newton on 25 April 1970. Linton's other display outfit was the station aerobatic team 'Ebor'. Those in authority were not happy with the alcoholic link to gin used by the previous teams and I have a vague idea that the rather cranky name was chosen by the wife of the station commander on the grounds that the general public would recognise a derivation of the Roman name for York. Common sense eventually prevailed and it was later renamed as the Linton Blades by March 1970, led by the 1966 Wright Jubilee Trophy winner, Sqn Ldr Bob Turner. With over 34 shows during the 1971 season, the team made its debut at Linton-on-Ouse on 28 April for visitors from the RAF Staff College. On 7 July, the team flew to Turin in northern Italy for a show in support of British Week at Carpi; a flight beset with problems when the Dominie aircraft, tasked with navigating the Jet Provosts to their destination, became 'lost' in cloud over the Alps. Despite being low on fuel, the aircraft were able to safely land at Turin and the season finally ended on 18 September with shows over Knavesmire, York, and at RAF Leuchars.

"I later became known at Boscombe Down for refusing to keep current on the Jet Provost. One day I was suddenly required to go to Holme-on-Spalding-Moor for a meeting regarding a trial to clear the Harrier Mk 4 for rapid rolling, as I was the Harrier Project test pilot. The only way to get there was by air, and the only aircraft available was the Jet Provost, on which I was not current. So I was allocated a current pilot to take me there. This pilot was Lt Cdr David Poole RN, a colleague and friend on the Sea Harrier team, who was known as 'Pooligan'. I just sat in the Jet Provost's right seat, and he did all the work. He did a typical 'Pooligan take-off' from Boscombe's main runway, energetically lifting off and rolling on a 45-degree bank to zip around ATC. All fun so far, but at this point he had a sudden medical problem and collapsed on the controls. I grabbed control and put the aircraft in a less challenging flight path so I could see what had happened to him. He raised his head off the control column with his eyes creased in a big grin and said, 'You're current!'"

AVM Chris Spence RAAF was an exchange pilot and spent several intensive weeks flying with No. 1 FTS at Linton-on-Ouse between 1981 and 1983, during which time he also flew the Vampire T.11 with the Vintage Pair display team:

"At the time, the RAF/RAAF CFS QFI exchange alternated between Valley (fast-jet background) and Leeming (other), with the RAF QFI always going to RAAF CFS at RAAF East Sale. I was posted on exchange to RAF CFS in July 1981 and my first flight was at Leeming in a Jet Provost T3A on 11 August 1981. I must admit coming from flying a Macchi MB-326H to Jet Provost Mk 3 was something of a shock: bicycle chain-operated canopy, not much thrust, no pressurisation and side-by-side seating. On the other hand, it was great for aerobatics. My first JP5A flight was on 19 August 1981 (with Mark Gilson) and was a much closer experience to the Macchi with increased thrust and pressurisation – although having MDC above me on the canopy was a first.

"Interestingly the RAAF and RAF QFI courses were very closely aligned although the emphasis in the RAF syllabus was rather more 'standardised'. I was signed up

Following his success at three aerobatic competitions, it was decided that Flt Lt David 'Duck' Webb, a QFI at No. 1 FTS, should form the Wright Jubilee Pair in 1977 with Sqn Ldr Eddie Danks flying a spare aircraft. (Wg Cdr Eddie Danks)

as C to I on 12 October 1981 and proceeded to No. 1 FTS at RAF Linton-on-Ouse in early November ostensibly to 'tick the box' on sending a trainee first solo on the JP3A. This may well have been because my instructing experience prior to RAAF CFS had been at our 'advanced' Flying Training School (2FTS) at Pearce rather than the ab-initio school (1FTS) at Point Cook. All the flights at Linton were on the JP3A and undertaken from 2 November to 27 November 1981 (a total of 25 flights).

"Back at No. 2 Jet Provost Squadron, CFS at Leeming, I went on to gain an RAF A2 on the Jet Provost on 6 September 1982 (followed by Command Examiner – the dreaded 'Trapper') on 20 January 1983 (having moved to Examining Wing). In the meantime, I qualified on the Vampire T.11 on 15 April 1982, the Bulldog on 18 January 1983 and the Chipmunk T.10 on 28 January 1983. Finally I was signed up as QFI/examiner on the Jet Provost, Bulldog and Chipmunk on 15 February 1983."

No story of Linton-on-Ouse in the mid-1970s would be complete without mentioning Flt Lt David 'Duck' Webb, a former Lightning pilot and a QFI with No. 2 Squadron, 1 FTS. In 1976 he successfully competed in three aerobatic competitions, which included the No. 1 FTS Competition to represent the station – the Jarvis Trophy, the Wright Jubilee Competition at RAF Cranwell, and the

Shell Embassy Competition at Greenham Common. **Sqn Ldr Eddie Danks** had been appointed to form No. 4 Squadron, 1 FTS, with the responsibility for arranging and conducting the aerobatic training for the Wright Jubilee Trophy competition at RAF Cranwell in May 1976:

> "'Duck' Webb was a most worthy winner of the Wright Jubilee Competition. We then worked up for the first-ever Shell Embassy International Air Tattoo Aerobatic Competition held at RAF Greenham Common over the weekend 29 July–2 August 1976. Duck put on a superb display against the top UK, European and American display pilots to win at such a prestigious event. It was then agreed that we should form the Wright Jubilee Pair, and that I would manage and lead (in the spare aircraft), while Duck would fly the solo aerobatic display. For the arrivals we could carry out looping split-breaks to land – as per Cranwell Poacher days in 1973. Duck also displayed at the Battle of Britain displays at St Athan and Jersey that year; at Jersey we flew with the Red Arrows and the Vintage Pair. The 'WJ' pair only lasted the one season as Duck did not compete in the pre-Wright Jubilee Competition in 1977 run-off for personal reasons."

MODIFICATIONS TO THE MK 5

The new redesigned front fuselage and pressurised cockpit of the T Mk 5 featured a power-operated, rearward-sliding canopy and two Martin-Baker Mk 4 ejection seats. In an emergency, the canopy was jettisoned automatically by explosive rams, which lifted the leading edge into the slipstream and allowed the airflow to take it upwards and over the fin. However, there was about a 0.5-second delay to allow the canopy to clear the fin and ensure the seat did not fire and hit the canopy. Although not long, 0.5 seconds was deemed too long to wait after pulling the handle before the seat fired and, in a critical situation, this could prove to be fatal.

In early 1968, the RAF requested the development of a seat and canopy removal system modified with a miniature detonation system (MDC), which incorporated a sheathed cord bonded to the inside of the Perspex canopy, a cartridge-firing unit behind each of the seats and a detonator system. Following a series of development trials by BAC at Warton and the A&AEE wind tunnel at Boscombe Down, the unacceptable delay in the canopy jettison sequence was eventually eliminated.

Jet Provost Mk 5 XW352 navigation training aircraft of No. 6 FTS RAF Finningley, also unofficially referred to as the 'Mk 5B'. (Ministry of Defence)

Dave Croser:

> "The original Jet Provost Mk 5s went into service without the MDC as the idea was fairly new, and it was not until a tasking was received from the MoD for BAC to undertake a trial. The tests were successful. The MDC shattered the canopy in less than 0.1 seconds and the seat firing was almost simultaneous after pulling the handle. We undertook trials to ensure that the canopy cleared the fin at all speeds, including in the spin. One could say that the spin was exciting without jettisoning the canopy in the middle of it."

Between June 1975 and March 1976, work to upgrade 61 Jet Provost Mk 5s with the installation of a seat and canopy removal system was carried out by a working party at RAF Leeming. Previously, a major modification programme to the RAF's Jet Provost fleet began when the first of 179 Jet Provost Mk 3 and Mk 5 aircraft were flown into Warton to be fitted with new radio and navigation equipment to meet the latest air traffic control requirements. Ninety-three Mk 5s were upgraded to Mk 5A standard between October 1973 and January 1976. The opportunity was also taken to revise the instrument layouts of both types of aircraft to introduce a greater commonality between the Mk 3A and Mk 5A.

From October to December 1975, an additional batch of 13 T Mk 5s was modified for use as long-range, low-level navigational trainers with No. 6 FTS at Finningley. The work undertaken at Leeming included removing the nose strakes and fitting 48-gallon tip tanks to enhance training sorties. Deliveries began in October 1975. In 1988, the wings of some of the aircraft began to fail the structural fatigue tests and five 'low fatigue' airframes were modified at Scampton as replacements; the upgraded airframes retained their wingtip tanks and nose strakes, and were unofficially known as 'T Mk 5Bs'.

RAF COLLEGE, CRANWELL 'GOLDEN EAGLE FLIGHT'

In the summer of 1970, Sqn Ldr Richard Johns, a squadron commander at the RAF College, Cranwell, was appointed as the jet-flying training instructor to HRH Charles, the Prince of Wales. The prince who joined No. 1 Graduate Entry in March 1971 had previously flown Chipmunk and Beagle Basset aircraft before arriving at Cranwell and was allocated two Jet Provosts, XW322 and 323, for his five-month course; codenamed 'Golden Eagle Flight', both aircraft had been delivered, as new, from Warton in December 1970. The aircraft would be maintained by a team of 15 selected ground crew and were subjected to strict security, being locked under guard in a hangar each night.

Following a period of ground-school training HRH began flying on 19 March 1971 and went solo after eight hours of instruction. **John Robinson** was the Golden Eagle Flight's deputy flying instructor:

> "The college was due to receive its first Jet Provost Mk 5s the end of 1970 and it fell to me to check out the aircraft as I had done the initial acceptance of them to the CFS. The work on the two aircraft involved some 200 flying hours and I carried out the acceptance air test on XW323 on 21 December 1970 and that on XW322 on 11 January 1971.

Two Jet Provosts of the Golden Eagle Flight flown by Sqn Ldrs Richard Johns and John Robinson during their acceptance checks between December 1971 and January 1972. (Ministry of Defence)

"There were no additional modifications to the aircraft for the purposes of the operation that I was aware of. The only thing that I can think of is that the aircraft and their Viper 204 variant engines were completed to a higher standard of inspection when being constructed than the normal 'off-the-line' aircraft.

"There was no specific date for me to become the deputy flying instructor to Sqn Ldr Dick Johns for the training of HRH and I had to fly with the CFS Examining Wing to verify my position on 16 February 1971. Dick carried out his initial training and I flew my first sortie with HRH on 29 April 1971, taking my turn throughout his training, which covered all aspects from the standard student pilot syllabus."

Prince Charles' total flying time for the course was just over 92 hours, of which 23½ were solo, and he completed his final handling test on 8 July 1971. The following month, the prince was awarded his wings from ACM Sir Denis Spotswood, chief of the Air Staff, at the passing out parade at Cranwell on 20 August 1971.

At the beginning of September 1976, the college was notified that Prince Charles was to return to Cranwell for a refresher course. By this time, Sqn Ldr Dick Johns

HRH Prince Charles with his instructor Sqn Ldr John Robinson and the ground crew of the reformed Golden Eagle Flight following his return to Cranwell for a refresher course. (via Brian Davies)

had been posted and Sqn Ldr John Robinson was left to organise his arrival, including collecting the two Golden Eagle Jet Provost Mk 5s from 5 MU at Kemble and re-establishing the previous security arrangements. Prince Charles received his first refresher flight on 23 October 1976, and after three days he transferred to RAF Valley for a familiarisation flight in a Hunter under the guidance of QFI, Flt Lt Peter Squire.

The two Jet Provosts were returned to No. 5 MU Kemble in February 1977.

Sean Chiddention was an instructor at the RAF College, Cranwell, and successfully competed in the Wright Jubilee Aerobatic Competition at RAF Valley on 15 May 1987. He was not only the youngest pilot to win the competition but also achieved the distinction of winning the trophy two years in succession:

"The competition was for all Jet Provost instructors from RAF Cranwell, Scampton, Finningley, Church Fenton and Linton-on-Ouse, with each station holding its own selection competition before the main event. The winner from each station went forward to compete in the Wright Jubilee competition, which was held at either Scampton or Valley, depending upon the weather on the day. The winner of the overall competition then went on to be the Jet Provost display pilot for the season.

"The 1987 event was held at Valley and I competed in XW335. I was fortunate to win and went on to become the youngest ever display pilot as a flying officer, aged 22. As a Cranwell instructor I was aware of the Poachers aerobatic team and elected to have both my aircraft (XW323 and XW374) painted in their colour scheme, complete with the traditional Cranwell blue band swept across the rear fuselage and tail, and on the wing undersides. The two aircraft were selected based on their low fatigue lives, both having been in storage early in their careers. One of these aircraft (XW323) had been flown by Prince Charles during his time at Cranwell in 1971.

"The first public display was just two weeks later at Prestwick. Through the season I flew 43 displays, mostly in XW374, with XW323 as the spare. Most weekends consisted of taking both aircraft, as a pair, using the call sign 'Poacher Formation', the second aircraft being flown by one of the other Cranwell instructors and each carrying a volunteer and hard-working engineer. The final display of the season was flown at Tours in France on 4 October, flown in XW323.

"In 1988, and still with sufficient time remaining of my 'creamy' tour, I managed to successfully defend my title and went on to display again for the 1988 season. The competition was again held at Valley on 10 May and I flew XW428, with a normal paint scheme in order not to pre-empt the outcome. The format for the display routine in 1988 was similar, with XW323 taking the lead role. The first display, of the 37 that season, was flown at Bournemouth on 4 June in XW323 and the last time was at RAF Newton on 18 September, again in XW323."

THE END IS NIGH?

Flt Lt Stevie Howard from No. 1 FTS Linton-on-Ouse was the last RAF pilot to officially demonstrate the Jet Provost:

"I won the Jarvis Aerobatic Competition on 20 November 1991 at Linton-on-Ouse and became the RAF Jet Provost display pilot for the 1992 summer season. I did about 36 solo aerobatic displays in the UK and Europe, with Flt Lt Gregg Hurst flying the spare aircraft and the coordination of all admin arrangements as the display manager.

"I believe that I was the last RAF pilot to demonstrate the Jet Provost and chose to fly the Mk 3 over the Mk 5A as it was better in the vertical and sharper at stall-turn manoeuvres, even though it had less thrust. I started the sequence at 300 kts after a 5,000-ft dive and it just about kept enough energy through the five-minute aerobatic routine.

"We used the formation call sign 'Blade' as we arrived and departed air shows as a pair, which was used as a nod to the days when 1 FTS had a formation display team called the Blades. That is why there was a '1' on the fin.

"Gregg Hurst flew a similarly painted spare aircraft in case mine had a technical issue, and when we arrived at air shows our party trick was to come in as low as possible in an exceedingly tight formation (i.e. overlapping wings). Sadly, Gregg was killed on 21 January 1999 in a mid-air collision with a Cessna near Mattersey, Notts, while flying a Tornado from RAF Cottesmore.

"The 'mirror image' photograph many will have seen was from a one-off photo shoot on 14 May with myself, Gregg and a third photo Jet Provost containing an RAF photographer [see plate section]. We were trying for the arrangement from 'Top Gun' but didn't quite get the shot. The authorising squadron leader had insisted on a very formal and slow manoeuvring procedure for safety and with only 30 seconds in the inverted position before the engine flamed out, we didn't quite get there.

"My last display was at RAF Valley on 2 October 1992. I don't think there was another RAF Jet Provost display pilot as it was during the transition to Tucano and Flt Lt Mark Discombe was the next RAF Linton-on-Ouse display pilot in that aircraft. I converted to the Tucano at Linton on 8 January 1993 but continued to fly Jet Provost 3 and Jet Provost 5 concurrently, which was a little mind-bending at times because the Tucano had a significantly different pilot training syllabus to that of the Jet Provost course. My last trip on the Jet Provost was in a Mk 5 on 17 June 1993, and my 'creamy' QFI tour came to an end in July 1993 when I resumed my Hawk weapons training at RAF Chivenor.

"I went on to fly over 2,000 hours on the Jaguar over nine years and I would be lying if I said that any other aircraft had greater hold over my affections. I do however keep very fond memories of the Jet Provost, largely thanks to that aerobatic season as it is very rare to be able to stall turn a jet-engined aircraft let alone perform complex stall-turn manoeuvres such as reverse stall turns, 'Noddy' stall turns and the 'Prince of Wales' stall turn. The sheer variety of manoeuvres available to the Jet Provost was way in excess of anything a faster front-line jet could perform."

In April 1992, No. 1 FTS became the last training school to receive the Short Tucano training aircraft; however, these aircraft would take longer to replace the Jet Provosts because of the large backlog of students waiting to progress for advanced training. As a result, the school's official retirement date for its Jet Provosts was deferred until 20 May 1993, when a formation of 14 aircraft were flown in the shape 'J' and P' over Linton-on-Ouse as a final tribute.

Gp Capt Paul McDonald was the CI/OC FTW at No. 1 FTS, Linton-on-Ouse between 1992 and 1994, to whom I am most grateful for the extract from his book *Winged Warriors* which detailed the event:

"Throughout May we also practised some slightly unusual formation flying for the formal date set for the retirement of the Jet Provost, 20 May 1993. The guest of honour would be AVM Coville. We planned to fly a formation over the airfield in the shape of the letters 'J' and 'P'. Sqn Ldr Mark Heaton was nominated as the overall formation leader and would lead the 'P' with me flying alongside him in line abreast. The squadron commander of Standards Squadron, Dave 'Cutty' Cuthbertson, would lead the 'J'.

"All of the rehearsals went well and the plan was to arrive over the saluting dais from the north-west. A number of photographs were taken during the rehearsals, which was just as well as 20 May was a grey day and the forecast was for a gradually reducing cloud base with an increasing likelihood of rain. While the forecast was marginal, it looked as if the very poor weather would hold off until about midday, so we all got airborne and formed up as we headed north-west. Timing had to be to the second, and, as we turned for the final time to commence our run, all looked good. Then the cloud began to lower.

"So we had to descend. In descending we began to accelerate, which we could not afford to do, otherwise we would have been much too early. We did not have enough time to turn around nor could such an unwieldy formation jink very much to the left or right to lose time. All Mark Heaton could do was to very gently throttle back, but this had to be done so carefully as speed changes tended to cascade back down the formation making it very difficult to hang on. It was harder for the formation alongside us and especially for those aircraft flying in line astern. We got lower and lower. Something had to give. And it did. It was Cutty. He simply said that he could no longer stay with us and he descended even lower to accelerate and make his formation more manageable before diverging away from us to the west. What a disaster I thought, but Cutty had no choice if he was to safely retain the integrity of his formation.

"I could see all of this unfold as I was on the port side of Mark as the 'J' began to move away. If we continued AVM Coville would be over flown by a 'P' only, which would have been awful. We were within seconds of calling the whole thing off when Cutty called that he was coming back in but he needed the formation leader to give him another ten knots. There he was, just skirting below low stratus cloud to the west moving closer and ever closer toward us. But we were also getting closer and closer to the airfield. Would the formation be back together before we reached the airfield boundary? Thankfully the weather helped. On the ground it had begun to rain heavily and the visibility was much reduced. Most people had sought shelter, but AVM Coville and the station commander remained to take the salute, with umbrellas raised. The 'JP' arrived exactly on time, in perfect formation, albeit significantly lower than planned."

On 22 July 1993, the Jet Provost Mk 3As were finally withdrawn from No. 1 FTS when the school's remaining aircraft were flown to Shawbury for disposal, led by Linton's station commander, Gp Capt Tom Eeles.

Paul McDonald was also involved in the disposal of the last Jet Provost sorties from Linton-on-Ouse:

"I had flown a number of final handling tests in April and May 1993 prior to the demise of the Jet Provost. In early July we were tasked to deliver a Jet Provost from storage at RAF Shawbury to the new owner, who was operating from the former RAF airfield at Binbrook. So, on 6 July 1994, I flew solo the very final sortie to be undertaken by the RAF in a Jet Provost Mk 5 A, XW336."

NO. 6 FTS/LOW LEVEL AIR DEFENCE TRAINING SQUADRON

Based at Finningley, the LLADTS retained its Jet Provosts in the navigation training role until 14 August 1993, when four aircraft were flown in a 'dying swan' formation over the airfield in company with four of the Hawk aircraft which had taken over their role. **Wg Cdr 'Jeff' Jefford**:

"The courses already in residence in the summer of 1992 stayed on the 'old' backward-facing Dominie/Jet Provost syllabus until they graduated a year later – so one needed the Jet Provost to remain until 1993 as you can't make a major change to a training sequence in mid-course. Any course that started later than the autumn of 1992 would have been on the new, streamed, fast jet vs heavy sequence. So there was a transition stage of about a year while both sequences ran in parallel, with the new one gradually replacing the old."

The following month – on 21 September 1993 – the squadron's last Jet Provosts (XW287, XW296, XW307 and XW429) were withdrawn, bringing an end to 23 years of specialised navigator training in the aircraft.

CHAPTER FOUR

LESSER-KNOWN JET PROVOST OPERATORS

THE CENTRAL AIR TRAFFIC CONTROL SCHOOL

Formed on 11 February 1963 from the Central Navigation and Control School at Shawbury, the CATCS provided live instruction for trainee air traffic controllers. Operated by Marshall's of Cambridge, the first two Jet Provost T Mk 4s (XR653 and XS219) were delivered on 24 August 1970, replacing its Vampire T.11s. In 1989 the CATCS switched to a purely computerised training programme and the Jet Provosts were withdrawn. To mark the occasion, on 5 July 1989 six aircraft (XP629, XP653, XP688, XR674, XS177 and XS181), led by the company test pilot Geoff Taylor, marked its official retirement with a 55-minute flypast over local airfields, including Shrewsbury, Sleap, Cosford, Atcham and Condover; the aircraft being subsequently transferred to the local maintenance unit for disposal, with the exception of XS177 which was flown to St Athan.

TACTICAL WEAPONS UNIT/'C' FLIGHT, NO. 79 (RESERVE) SQUADRON

Following the disbandment of No. 229 OCU at Chivenor in September 1974, its task had been transferred to the newly formed Tactical Weapons Unit at Brawdy, commanded by Gp Capt Phil Champniss. The move to Brawdy coincided with the

Disbandment photograph of Central Air Traffic Control School at Shawbury in August 1970. (CATCS)

delivery of two Jet Provost T Mk 3s, XM579 and XN584, which were initially used by the pilots assigned to the Joint Forward Air Control Training and Standards Unit (JFACTSU), assisted by those of the TWU Standards Flight to support the training of RAF and army forward air controllers. In addition, the aircraft were used to provide UK Orientation Courses (UKOC) for foreign exchange pilots and ad hoc short refreshers for RAF pilots prior to their TWU course on the Hunters of No. 79(R) Squadron. In July 1978 the unit was renamed No. 1 TWU, with a second unit – No. 2 TWU – being established at RAF Lossiemouth in September and operating with Hunters as an interim measure until Chivenor was reactivated.

Dave McIntyre was posted to Brawdy in August 1981 to command 'C' Flight, No. 79 (R) Squadron:

> "When the fast-jet refresher students were sent to the RFS at Leeming in 1980, they complained that the 30-hour course was more than they needed, especially since they had all flown the Hunter. So by mid-1981, the MoD started sending them all directly to Brawdy, as well as the UKOC guys.
>
> "However, it must have become apparent that the 'refreshers' who were mostly senior officers, and had been on the ground for more than three or four years, were having difficulty with simple things like working the radio and adjusting to

being back in the air, and they were arriving in sufficient numbers to overload the Standards team who had better things to do. In addition, the JFACTSU pilots were not best equipped to provide a standard course, partly because they weren't QFIs and they had their own tasking to consider, which frequently meant the TWU students were left to kick their heels for a week or two which was the last thing they needed.

"That was why the decision was made to formalise the Jet Provost refreshers and bring it 'in house' to No. 79 (R) Squadron. The problem was not airframe hours, it was pilot availability. Since the ten-hour syllabus was much the same for the foreigners and for refreshers, it made sense to formalise it. RAF pilots who had been on the ground for a single tour went straight to the Hunter, but any longer than that and they got their ten hours of 'no pressure' flying on the Jet Provost. This proved to be very effective as they were able to maximise their time on the TWU course rather than spend the first few hours struggling to regain their previous confidence. Most of them confessed to some trepidation at being asked to do too much, too soon.

"Unlike most of the sources, I can confirm that certainly after August 1981 when 'C' Flight No. 79 (R) Squadron was formed at Brawdy, although the Jet Provosts were used for FAC training, they did not belong to JFACTSU exclusively and used them only when needed. When I arrived, the three on unit strength were still XP547, XP564 and XS178, and as I was on my own, it didn't restrict the periodic demands of the FAC courses. After I ejected in April 1982 (in XP564), Herbie Sutcliffe was posted in at short notice, and whilst I was still recovering it was replaced by XR679. By the time I was fit to fly again, the demand increased so the two of us were kept pretty busy. By November 1982, XS219 arrived to bring the unit establishment up to four, and apart from the occasional loan from Shawbury, they formed the fleet until they were retired."

Initially, the two Jet Provost T Mk 4s retained their original red and white training colours, but in May 1976 they were repainted in a tactical camouflage scheme to provide more realism in the FAC role; the first aircraft to be repainted being XP547. **Dave McIntyre** again:

"As the camouflaged Jet Provosts were a curiosity, they were popular on the static line at air shows around the country, but after the last of the Hunters were retired to St Athan on 26 July 1984, the days of the Jet Provost were numbered. Unlike the

Air defence grey and tactical camouflage colour schemes worn by the Jet Provost Mk 4s of No. 79 (R) Squadron, No. 1 TWU at RAF Brawdy in 1987. (Geoff Lee via Bill Perrins)

BFTS Jet Provosts/Tucanos, the sortie endurance at Brawdy was not an issue, but using them as a TWU lead-in became less relevant, in addition to creating servicing and spares difficulties. The Hawks could do the job more efficiently so the surprise is that the Jet Provosts lasted as long as they did."

By 1989, it had been decided to retire the unit's Jet Provosts. To mark the occasion, four aircraft (XP547/0, XR679/04, XS178/05 and XS219/06) flown by Flt Lt Clive Carnazza, Flt Lt Ashley Frost, Sqn Ldr John Webb from 79 Squadron and Flt Lt Pat Wareham from JFACTSU, made a farewell sortie over St David's Cathedral, Fishguard, Aberporth, the Sennybridge Range, Haverfordwest and Milford Haven on 22 March. The aircraft were finally flown to RAF Cosford as ground instructional airframes on 31 March 1989.

No. 26 Squadron was reformed in February 1969 from the Southern Communication Squadron at RAF Wyton. Operating a mix of light aircraft including Basset CC.1s and Devon C.2s, its primary function was to ferry RAF Training Command staff officers and crews, and in July 1974 the squadron took delivery of two Jet Provost T Mk 3s (XM453 and XM455) for continuation training. Following a re-organisation of the numbered communication squadrons, the squadron was disbanded in April 1976.

JET PROVOST TRIALS UNIT (FAR EAST)

Between 1963 and 1966, the Indonesian Confrontation was a violent conflict that stemmed from the creation of the Federation of Malaysia and which reached its climax in 1962. With air operations being a major part of the campaign, RAF close air support for ground army units operating in the forward jungle areas was essential.

At this time, the RAF had very little experience of operations of this nature over Malaysia and Singapore, which resulted in the JPTU(FE) being formed in August 1965 to examine forward air control (FAC) operations over this type of terrain. Based at Tengah and equipped with three Jet Provost T Mk 4s, the unit was initially commanded by Sqn Ldr Mick Ryan and included Flt Lts Roy Holmes and Bob Innes, both with ground-attack experience. The three officers were joined later by Sqn Ldr George Ord, another experienced ground-attack pilot, together with a team of scientists which included Roger Noades, who was attached to the unit to set the daily tasks.

The unit's dismantled Jet Provosts (XS221, XS223 and XS224) had been flown out to Seletar by three Argosy transport aircraft and arrived at Changi on 15 August 1965; the aircrew flew out to Singapore separately by Comet aircraft and were later joined by a volunteer ground crew. On arrival at Changi, the Jet Provosts were transported by road to Seletar and re-assembled, with XS224 being air tested by Sqn Ldr Ryan on 28 August and flown to RAF Tengah. The aircraft were specially modified for the trial, which involved the fitting of special Hussenot recorder units in the rear fuselage, together with gunsights and GR.90 gun cameras; items not fitted to the standard Jet Provost. Also fitted were PTR 175 combined VHF/UHF radios to ensure full communication with the ground units.

Trials began with selected, transportable target areas in the jungle of the southern Malaysia Peninsula which entailed the pilots flying to the general area of the target, looking for a Day-Glo red balloon flying above the jungle canopy, which indicated the FAC's position. The task set by Roger Noades was for six details a day, involving two aircraft and 30 runs per aircraft. A major concern for Mick Ryan during the trials was 'target fixation', as it would have been possible for one of the pilots, in the enthusiasm of trying to bring back successful pictures of the target to forget about pull-out heights. However, there was one serious incident when one of the pilots climbing gently away from an attack failed to see a lone tree standing above the jungle canopy but below the jungle skyline.

Although the pilot flew through the top of the tree he was able to get his aircraft back to Tengah, where the damaged wing was replaced. **Wg Cdr Mick Ryan**:

> "The scientists were forever wanting more runs at all the combinations to make their figures more reliable, and as far as I can remember, it was Bob Innes who flew through the treetop in XS224. It required a main wing change which would normally make it a Category 3 and therefore a recordable accident. However, as we could order a replacement wing and had the staff and knew how to fit it, it was only classified as a Cat 2. That could have been the period of repair but do not know on which day it occurred, possibly from 18 October to 4 November."

On 11 October 1965, having exhausted the suitable target areas in the south of the peninsula, the unit departed for RAAF Butterworth as the terrain was considered the most representative of the Borneo jungle. Here, a FAC team was deployed into the mountainous jungle that runs along the central spine of the peninsula, with each team again setting up six targets a day. One of the original aims of the trial was for the unit to deploy to Borneo and fly over the terrain that the main part of the confrontation was being fought in. As this idea did not go down well with the units on the ground in Borneo, Mick Ryan flew into Kuching, Sarawak, instead to assess if the terrain in Central Malaysia was comparable to that in Borneo. These flights were in Single and Twin Pioneer aircraft and gave him the opportunity to study the terrain at first hand. After several days of flights over Sarawak, Mick Ryan was able to confirm that the terrain in the areas that the unit was using for training in West Malaysia were very representative of the type of terrain in the area of operations. Therefore there was no need for the Trials Unit to deploy the 400-plus nautical miles to Kuching.

Mick Ryan again:

> "I was flown down to Changi on 17 November and returned on 22 November. That seems to be the only period I was away from the trial and I would have had to go to Borneo from Changi using RAF transport. I know that when I got there, my old wing commander flying from Jever (a hairy, grizzled Australian – Geoff Atherton) greeted me off the transport and promptly told me to 'f*** off', as they seemed to think they had a war on their hands and they could do without Jet Provosts. Thus I was just allowed to fly as a passenger on various Single and Twin Pioneer supply

The personnel of the Jet Provost Trials Unit commanded by Sqn Ldr John Harvey at RAAF Butterworth in February 1966. (via Keith Gainey)

runs and a few helicopter missions. Enough to get a good feel for the land and agree that the spine of Malaysia was very similar."

All the tasks were completed by the unit by November, and on 30 November 1965 the three aircraft were returned to No. 389 MU at Seletar for storage; the air and ground crews departed to the UK shortly after.

During February 1966 the trial was resurrected to examine further FAC combinations and techniques. Commanded by Sqn Ldr John Harvey, the first two aircraft, XS221 and XS224, were withdrawn from storage on 1 February and reissued to the Trials Unit; the third aircraft, XS223, followed two weeks later. Operating from Butterworth, the Jet Provosts were active with a number of FAC missions over the Nami, Fort Baling and Krian regions of Malaysia. On 5 February 1966, the trials were quickly halted with the tragic loss of Flt Lt Pete Loveday in XS221, which crashed near Alor Star, Malaya, after hitting a tall tree and ripping the wing off.

As a result, the second trial was wound up on 14 March 1966 with the remaining two aircraft being returned again to store at No. 389 MU, Seletar. From there, they went back to the UK and No. 27 MU. In January 1967, they were sold back to BAC and converted into the armed export version of the Jet Provost for the Yemeni air force.

Keith Gainey was a member of both trials:

"I was based at Linton-on-Ouse at the time which had Jet Provosts and volunteered for the Far East trials. During the first set of trials, we assembled the Jet Provosts at Changi and then went to Seletar for the flying trials, before moving to Tengah.

Following the first trial we dismantled the Jet Provosts and boxed them up as we did not know there was going to be a second trial. One of the Jet Provosts required some engine work before flying to RAAF Butterworth, so only two aircraft and most of the ground crew then flew up to Butterworth. A chief tech, myself and engine fitter stayed behind and carried out the repairs. We then travelled to Penang by the railway which had been built by the POWs in the war."

NO. 3/4 CIVILIAN ANTI-AIRCRAFT COOPERATION UNIT

Operated by Airwork Services at Exeter Airport, No. 3/4 CAACU was primarily engaged in target towing for all three services. Equipped with a successive variety of aircraft, they were also used for simulated shipping attacks and as radar targets. By April 1958 the unit was equipped with Vampires and Meteors until 31 December 1971, when its duties were taken over by the newly reformed No. 7 Squadron at St Mawgan equipped with Canberra TT.18s and it was disbanded.

Between April 1969 and July 1970, four Jet Provosts were issued to the unit at different periods and used in a 'Vampire Evaluation Trial'.

Local aviation historian, **Alistair Henderson**, commented on the existence of the Jet Provosts at Exeter Airport:

"It seems odd that their presence at the CAACU was barely recorded, and that a Vampire replacement was even contemplated so near to its disbandment. Jet Provost XS177 would seem to have been the first to be operated in April 1969, while the next one (XR643) didn't arrive until December. They would mostly fly from Monday to Friday, and even then, not every day."

The Jet Provosts involved in the evaluation were:

XR643: coded 'DJW' (Flt Lt John Willison, Wright Jubilee winner in 1969). It was issued to 3/4 CAACU Exeter for the Vampire replacement evaluation on 5-12-69. Then to 5 MU at Kemble on 10-1-70 as unit test pilot's aircraft and hack.
XS177: to 3/4 CAACU on 1-4-69. To 3 FTS coded '43' on 8-7-69.
XR679: to 3/4 CAACU from CAW Manby coded '21' on 19-2-70 and returned to Manby still coded '21' on 1-5-70.
XP558: to 3/4 CAACU on 22-1-70. It then went to CAW Manby coded '20' on 9-7-70, where it went on to fly with the Macaws display team in 1973.

LESSER-KNOWN JET PROVOST OPERATORS

Between 1973 and 1974, former RAF display pilot Bob Thompson (at rear) went on to partner Tom Maloney in several civilian display teams. (Bob Thompson)

CIVILIAN DISPLAY FLYING

Following their withdrawal from service, at least 112 Jet Provost and Strikemaster aircraft were sold to private buyers in the UK, USA, Canada and Australia for private flying or to display on the air-show circuit. The following are just a few examples of the operator/owners.

BOB THOMPSON

Following a successful aerobatic display career with the RAF's the Gemini Pair and the Swords between 1973 and 1974, **Bob Thompson** went on to partner Tom Maloney in several civilian display teams:

> "I flew with the Transair Jet Provost Duo during 1976/77, and the renamed Strikemaster Duo in 1978. I continued to give solo displays in a wide range of jet and piston aircraft and helicopters until my air display retirement on 6 February 2003. I had spent 38 years and 1,865 hours flying both the Jet Provost and the Strikemaster in Europe, USA, Africa and the Middle East."

JP Mk 3 – XM351 – 23 February 1965 – RAF Church Fenton Basic Training
JP Mk 4 – XR646 – 23 July 1965 – RAF Church Fenton Basic Training
JP Mk 5 – XW293 – 2 November 1970 – CFS RAF Little Rissington Central Flying School Instructor Course
JP Mk 3A – XM459 – 16 January 1975 – RAF Leeming – Basic Flying Instructor Tour
JP Mk 5A – XW310 – July 1975 – RAF Leeming – Basic Flying Instructor Tour
JP Mk 5B – XW304 – 13 November 1975 – RAF Leeming – Basic Flying Instructor Tour
JP Mk 52 – G-PROV – 12 March 1993 – Bournemouth
Strikemaster Mk 87 – G-AYHR – 7 March 1998 – North Weald
Strikemaster Mk 83 – G-BXFV – 18 May 2001 – Humberside
JP Mk 1 – G-AOBU – 19 June 2001 – Cranfield – (Displayed Filton 23 Jul 2001)
Last Strikemaster Flight – G-BXFP – 6 February 2003 – Chalgrove to Humberside – Aircraft sale/delivery
Last Jet Provost Flight – G-BWOT – 15 September 2003 – Kemble

Memorable Jet Provost Flying

26 May 1993–28 May 1993 – Jet Provost Mk 4 – G-JETP – Ferry flight Bournemouth to Paphos Cyprus – Aircraft delivery flight – Returned 29 September–5 October 1993 to conduct JP type rating training for Cypriot pilots.

JEFF BELL

The owner of XW324/G-BWSG:

"Prior to purchasing my Jet Provost in November 2007, I was just an ordinary air show punter watching and enjoying from the crowd side of the fence like everyone else. I was in the air cadets and frequently went to our local RAF Finningley air show with the squadron doing the usual stuff like car park duty, selling programmes and the ubiquitous litter pick following the show. I guess I always daydreamed that one day I'd be the other side of the fence taking part but viewed that ambition as purely a pipe dream, that was until 2007 when this literally took off.

"It all started back in September 2001 at the time the Twin Towers in New York were hit. I was actually attending the NBAA aviation convention in New Orleans which was subsequently cancelled and left us with nothing to do but tour the city,

ABOVE: *Seen during the extensive flight trials, XD674 was relegated as an instructional airframe in 1958 and eventually became a part of the historic aircraft collection at the RAF Museum at Cosford. (BAe Systems Heritage Warton-Percival/Hunting Collection)*

BELOW: *Flt Lts 'Curly' Hirst and Jimmy Rhind of the CFS Jet Provost synchronised display team 'The Redskins' in 1959.*

ABOVE: *The RAF's premier display team in 1964. Six CFS Jet Provosts of 'The Red Pelicans' from RAF Little Rissingon. (BAe Systems Heritage Warton-Percival/Hunting Collection)*

LEFT: *Originally formed to provide flypasts at graduation days, the Cranwell Jet Provosts of 'The Poachers' made its first official display in December 1963. By April 1969, the renamed 'Cranwell Poachers' assumed a greater display commitment under the leadership of Sqn Ldr Bill Jago.*

The first official four-ship (albeit short-lived) Jet Provost station team led by Flt Lt John Spreadbury from No. 2 FTS at RAF Syerston in 1961. (Author)

ABOVE: *High above the Lincolnshire Wolds, the CAW Macaws. (Ministry of Defence)*

BELOW: *The last Jet Provost display team to be formed from No. 1 FTS Linton-on-Ouse was The Vipers in 1969, led by Sqn Ldr John Merry. (Ministry of Defence)*

The Central Flying School Aerobatic Team in July 1960. (BAe Systems Heritage Warton-Percival/Hunting Collection)

ABOVE: *Displaying its trademark formation 'mirror' manoeuvre, Flt Lt Gordon Revell and Fg Off Ron Pattinson of Gemini Pair formate with a Harrier from Wittering in July 1970. (Ron Pattinson)*

BELOW: *The conclusion of a routine featured by the Macaws team was a 'petal break', seen here at Biggin Hill in 1968. (Peter Cowen)*

ABOVE: *The Gemini Pair in Jet Provost T Mk 4s over the North Yorkshire Moors in 1970.*

BELOW: *The Gemini display team at Cameri, northern Italy in May 1973. From left to right standing: Sqn Ldr Olly Knight (manager), Fg Off 'Dusty' Miller (Gemini 2), Flt Lt Brian Fuller (commentator), Flt Lt 'Bob' Thompson (Gemini 1), and Wg Cdr Robin Blockley (chief instructor). Kneeling: SAC Ron Anderson and SAC Bob Goodier. (Olly Knight)*

Seen from the cockpit of the inverted Jet Provost during the trademark 'Roulette' manoeuvre, XW332 of the No. 3 FTS display team in 1971. (Ron Pattinson)

ABOVE: *The morning flightline of No. 1 FTS of RAF Linton-on-Ouse in 1978, with Jet Provost T Mk 4s and T Mk 5s. (Ministry of Defence)*

BELOW: *A formation of Jet Provosts of No. 79 (R) Squadron, No. 1 TWU in a tactical camouflage scheme practising their 'Viper Red Formation' over St Bride's Bay on 21 July 1986 for an air day at RAF Brawdy. (Ian Black via Dave McIntyre)*

ABOVE: *The technical and administrative support staff behind the display team at RAF Manby. (Ministry of Defence)*

BELOW: *Flt Lt Steve Howard of No. 1 FTS was the solo display pilot from Linton-on-Ouse, with a reserve aircraft flown by Flt Lt Greg Hurst in May 1992. (MoD)*

ABOVE: *Strikemaster Mk 82 '404' of No. 1 (Strike) Squadron, flown by Russ Peart over the Salalah Plain. Between 1972 and 1974 he took part in 200 operational sorties against the rebel insurgents. (via Russ Peart)*

BELOW: *A formation of RSAF Strikemaster Mk 80As from the King Faisal Air Academy at Riyadh. (BAe Systems Heritage Warton-Percival/Hunting Collection)*

Taken during a high-level practice over Changi Airbase in 1978, the SADC's 'Synchro Pair' flown by Lt Fernandez (lead) and Capt Micky Liew. (Bruce Byron)

ABOVE: *First production Strikemaster Mk 88, NZ6361 for the RNZAF in May 1972. Delivered to Ohakea the following October, it served with No.14 (F) Squadron until December 1992. (BAe Systems Heritage Warton-Percival/Hunting Collection)*

BELOW: *The first Strikemaster Mk 83s of the Botswana Defence Force were delivered in March 1988. (BAe Systems Heritage Warton-Percival/Hunting Collection)*

ABOVE: *In January 2013, Jet Art Aviation at Selby acquired a number of Jet Provost T Mk 5As which had been used as maintenance training airframes at RAF Cosford. At least seven were eventually sold to foreign buyers. (Jet Art Aviation)*

BELOW: *Former Saudi Air Force Strikemaster Mk 80A G-RSAF '417', repainted in the colours of the Sultan of Oman Air Force and displayed by Strikemaster Display UK for the 2018 air display season. (Jamie Hunter via Strikemaster Display Team)*

ABOVE: *A 'Classic Jet Aircraft Association' formation in 2022. The lead aircraft was flown by Chris 'Neo' Lamprecht followed by Jimmy 'Purple' Hayes and Richard 'Dawg' Dawe in Jet Provost Mk 5, XW287. (Gary Daniels)*

BELOW: *Jet Provost Mk 3A N57553/XN553. (Alex Brancaccio)*

ABOVE: *A dramatic backdrop to an air show in Davenport, Iowa, called 'Red Star and The Dragon' – a simulated Vietnam-era dogfight between Strikemaster N6364Z 'Dragon 1' and an L-29 Delfin. (Andy Anderson)*

BELOW: *Reunion of the 1969 Red Pelicans team in Alderney, June 2022. From left to right: Tony Davies (No. 2), Richard Mackenzie-Crookes (No. 3), Rod Clayton (No. 4) John Robinson (No. 1) and John Davy (No. 5). (Sqn Ldr John Robinson)*

in a small place like New Orleans that only takes a day or two so we decided to see if we could get a flight over to Orlando.

"Having acquiesced to my other half's want and desire to do a week of the Disney Parks, I eventually got my chance to do something I wanted and we went initially to Tom Riley's Warbird Restoration Workshops then on to 'Warbird Adventures', both based at Kissimmee Municipal Airport. I then signed up and flew a Warbird Adventure SNJ-5 and later AT-6D Texans, which is what reignited my inner aviator.

"Upon my return to the UK I reviewed the possibility of purchasing and operating a T-6, or in British parlance, a Harvard only to find the cost was way beyond anything I could justifiably afford and the idea somewhat died there and then. A considerable time thereafter a copy of my monthly *Flypast* fell on the hall carpet with the cover page headline: 'Owning and operating the cheapest ex-military jet'.

"This led to a visit to RAF Cosford with a view to buying one of their Jet Provost 5 disposals, sadly all were really beyond economical recovery to service, again the idea died. Several months later, I received a call out of the blue asking if I was still trying to find a good airworthy Jet Provost 5? This turned out to be XW324 and following a visual inspection and associated negotiations I officially bought her on 27 September 2007.

"Work was needed to bring her back to flight status and I opted to upgrade her braking system to that of the Strikemaster at the same time. Once the work was completed, I and Sqn Ldr Dan Arlett ferried XW324 to her current home at East Midlands Airport on 25 May 2008.

Jet Provost Mk 5 XW324/G-BWSG in the colours of No. 6 FTS at RAF Valley in 2014. (Jeff Bell)

"We fly with Ollie Suckling, Mark Petrie, Chris Heames and others, and have also flown as a Strikemaster/Jet Provost Pair a few times as a three-ship and on one occasion a four-ship. To be fair, I don't personally display XW324, as I leave the display flying to those more eminently qualified to do so, either current serving or retired RAF crews; my rationale is that XW324 is safer in their capable hands."

STRIKEMASTER DISPLAY UK

Flown by Mark Petrie, former RAFO Strikemaster Mk82A, G-SOAF (ex-RAFO) '425' is one of the Strikemasters and Jet Provosts maintained by North Wales Military Aviation Service (NWMAS) at Hawarden and displayed by Strikemaster Display UK. For the 2018 air display season, G-SOAF was joined by former Saudi Mk 80A G- RSAF '417', which had been repainted in the colours of the Sultan of Oman Air Force and displayed with smoke at numerous air displays in the UK, Ireland and Europe. Until 2022, Ollie Suckling flew as his No. 2 for the synchronised displays or occasionally completed solo displays in G-RSAF or Jet Provost Mk 3 BKOU/XN637. Also in 2022, G-RSAF was used for training in support of 'Aero Legends' at North Weald for their new venture, 'Jet Legends' with a planned operations start in early 2023. G-RSAF will be leased to Jet Legends

Former Saudi Air Force Strikemaster Mk 80A G-RSAF '417' repainted in the colours of the Sultan of Oman Air Force and displayed by Strikemaster Display UK for the 2018 air display season. (Jamie Hunter via Strikemaster Display Team)

to support their operations from 2023 but will also continue to be used in air displays by Strikemaster Display UK.

SWORDS AVIATION

A 'Jet Pilot Training and Flying School', based at North Weald operates the only airworthy Jet Provost Mk 52. Originally built as a Mk 4 at Warton in 1964, it was delivered to the RAF as XS228 in July 1964 and returned to BAC in January 1967 for modification to Mk 52 standard as a ground-attack aircraft for export. The aircraft served with the South Arabian Federation (South Yemen) Air Force as '104' and saw active service until it was transferred to the Singapore Air Force in December 1975, when it was renumbered '352'. The aircraft was withdrawn from service in 1981 before being sold to the Hunter One Collection at North Weald in 1983 and placed on the civil register as G-PROV.

In March 2020 the school announced the launch of 'Jet Legends', their 'Top Gun' style, ex-military jet training and flying experience brand. Working closely with North Wales Military Aviation Services, the company also operates Strikemaster 'G-RSAF' from their base at North Weald Airfield, initially for type experience flights and full conversion courses to type, which commenced in late May 2022.

BLUE AIR TRAINING

In 2011 the Strikemaster was given a new lease of life when Blue Air Training, based at Las Vegas, Nevada, was formed to provide close air support training to conventional and special operations personnel from all branches of military service. With qualified reserve and air guard instructor pilots and forward air controllers, Blue Air Training's variety of dedicated aircraft included a number of Strikemaster aircraft, which were shared with its parent company. These included N702MF (a Mk 80 ex-Saudi 1104); N72445 (Mk 84 ex-Singapore AF 314); N358FS (Mk 88 ex-New Zealand NZ6361); N167BA (Mk 88 ex-New Zealand NZ6362); NZ6364Z (Mk 88 ex-NZ6374 on lease); N187BA (Mk 88 ex-New Zealand NZ6370). A further aircraft, (a Mk 80A, NZ605GV ex-Saudi 1114), crashed on 21 April 2017 and was written off. In addition, the company also operated a former RAF Jet Provost T Mk 5A, N556A/XW429, which was acquired in April 2015 for crew training. The company ceased Strikemaster operations in May 2020, with the aircraft being placed into storage and offered for sale.

Andy Anderson started flying with Blue Air Training when he stopped performing at air shows:

"I leased NZ6364/N6364Z aka 'The Dragon' and flew for them as an instructor pilot and sensor operator from 2017 to 2020. I instructed both the pilots and the maintenance people on how to maintain the aircraft. The Strikemasters used by Blue Air were fully re-armed with 7.62-mm machine guns and bomb capabilities, which we used on about half of the missions.

"The company's Jet Provost Mk 5 N556A/XW429 was never armed. When I got there, she had only flown a few times due to serious brake problems, which had become warped from overheating. I rebuilt them and flew her but she was never used as the trainer she was bought for. I think they were concerned about the lack of power.

"The company stopped flying the Strikemasters in 2020 as it was becoming too difficult to keep them flying due to a lack of parts, mainly brakes and starter generators. It's easy to keep one flying but seven was a challenge."

DONDI PESQUERA

Dondi first flew in a Jet Provost T4 (XP547/N547XP) during 2002, following which he became type-rated in both the Jet Provost and BAC-167 Strikemaster in 2007:

"I acquired my personal Jet Provost T Mk 5A (N326GV/XW326) in July 2012 and have been flying it non-stop for the last 11 years. My Jet Provost is hangared at the Zephyrhills, Florida airport, but I'm based in San Juan, Puerto Rico.

"I was eventually recognised by the Federal Aviation Administration (FAA) and the International Council of Air Shows (ICAS) as the first and only Puerto Rican pilot to ever hold an FAA/ICAS/EAA (Experimental Aircraft Association) Statement of Aerobatic Competency Low Level II (250 ft/air show license) (SAC Card). In total I have flown nearly 5,000 hours in over 80 different aircraft, including the A5 Super Decathlon, Christen Eagle, Marchetti SF.260, Van's RV-8, L-16 Luscombe, Stearman PT-17, T-6 Texan, T-34 Mentor, T-28 Trojan, P-40 Warhawk, P-51 Mustang, Fouga Magister, Jet Provost, L-39 Albatros, BAC-167 Strikemaster, MiG-15 and F-104 Starfighter."

Strikemaster aircraft at the busy flight line of Blue Air Training at Pensacola in Florida for live fire-training exercises for JTAC students. (Andy Anderson)

ANDY ANDERSON – 'DRAGON AVIATION', WILMINGTON, DELAWARE

Andy has owned three Strikemasters:

"I first bought N2146J (ex-Singapore AF) from a friend in 2006, the second was N167SM (ex-Yemen AF, which unfortunately crashed in the Hudson River, NY, in February 2011) and the one I still own is N6364Z (ex-RNZAF NZ6364). I still operate 'Dragon Aviation', and when the Strikemaster was owned by my friend he wanted nose art painted on her. We both decided that the old P-40 shark mouth was over-used. So we came up with the idea of a dragon's mouth, which eventually morphed into the dragon's head. She was simply referred to as 'The Dragon' by everyone after she was painted. The name stuck and was actually a great air show act name. The tail markings on 'Dragon 1' were from a Vietnam squadron operating out of Da Nang and were used because we had a Vietnam theme to the air show act. 'Dragon 2' was just made up to look good and 'Dragon 3' was from another air force squadron from Vietnam."

RICHARD DAWE

is based at Melbourne Municipal Airport in Arkansas:

"I flew Grumman EA-6B Prowlers during my career in the US Navy, and in 2019 I purchased my Jet Provost Mk 5 (N287XW/XW287) in Texas, making the transition

In August 2011, Dondi Pesquera was type-rated on both the Jet Provost and BAC 167 Strikemaster and later bought Jet Provost Mk 5A N326GV (ex-XW326) in Puerto Rico. (Dondi Pesquera)

from L-29s, Vampires, etc. I fly XW287 regularly and enjoy demonstrating it for the air show visitors and sharing the aircraft history with them."

DAVID WARREN

operates XW295, which is registered in Australia as VH-JPV and currently flown only by the owner and Jethro Nelson (ex-RAF):

"I bought Jet Provost, XW295, from Hugh Waltho of Essendon (Melbourne, Australia) in July 2015. It was he who had her painted silver and yellow – I don't know why? I would rather it was in correct colours, but it's rather a good paint job. Hugh spent a lot of money on restoration and avionics. XW295 is based and operated from Hobart Airport in Tasmania, and is IFR equipped. The registered operator is Zentel Aviation Pty Ltd and is wholly owned by myself. We display it at air shows, either static or flight display, and in the event that we have an active flight display, Jethro Nelson flies it, as he is ex-RAF and fully qualified with all the necessary tickets in Australia. I have taken her to Avalon Air Show (Australia's biggest military event) for static display, and also to Sydney Air Show (Illawarra) where we have flown active displays."

LESSER-KNOWN JET PROVOST OPERATORS

Former RNZAF Strikemaster Mk 88 NZ6364/NZ6364Z 'Dragon Three' of Dragon Aviation owned by Andy Anderson and operated from Smyrna, Tennessee. (Andy Anderson)

CHARLES DAVIES

"Strikemaster NZ6372/ZK-BAC was purchased by 'RNZAF Strikemaster Ltd' Auckland in March 2014 and previously operated by the Royal New Zealand Air Force from 1975 until 1992. It was one of 16 aircraft flown by No. 14 Squadron and today it remains the only ex-RNZAF Strikemaster flying in New Zealand. The aircraft is based at Wellington International Airport and regularly appears at air shows; it is also used for private flights on a cost/share basis. The two main pilots are myself and a retired Cathay Pacific captain, Dave Brown, who is the CFI for NZ Warbirds and flew A-4K Skyhawks with No. 75 Squadron; he was also the Strikemaster display pilot in 1988 and 1989."

Jet Provost Mk 5A XW295.

Dave Brown also flies a former RSAF Strikemaster Mk80A, '1130', at Christchurch, New Zealand. The aircraft is owned by **Brian Hall**:

"My Strikemaster was in service with the RSAF for 20 years, one of a second batch going into service in 1976 and based at the King Faisal Air Academy in Riyadh. When I purchased the aircraft in May 2011 it had been recently repainted in its original markings and I believe in retaining as much originality as possible. The Strikemaster is based at Christchurch International Airport and we have taken part in local displays in our area and at aviation gatherings, but not at air shows as such. We occasionally appear at 'Warbirds Over Wanaka', along with my T-28 Trojan. The main pilot is my engineer Kevin Langford, ex-Air New Zealand."

Strikemaster Mk 88 ZK-BAC/NZ6372 owned by Charles Davies, a Wellington-based surgeon. (via Brett Nicholls)

CHAPTER FIVE
RANDOM JET PROVOST MEMORIES

Allan Corkett was an instructor on the Jet Provost Mk 1 at Hullavington between 1955 and 1957:

"One of our serious problems came to light at the relief landing ground at Keevil. I had positioned my aircraft on the grass alongside the runway prior to demonstrating to my pupil a short take-off, as we were waiting for another Jet Provost to land. It touched down, and as it passed my aircraft its undercarriage collapsed. The aeroplane gyrated behind us on one wingtip, almost completing the circle and finishing with its wingtip just behind mine. Having noted from the aircraft's letter who the instructor was, I called over the RT: 'Good afternoon, Dougie.' It was Flt Lt T.C. Douglas. I heard his reply, ' ...and a good afternoon to you Allan' just as I switched my engine off and went to his assistance. The leg pivot was later redesigned and fitted to all aircraft without further problems."

Bob Osborne was critical of the standard of some flying instructors:

"Looking back on our times at basic flying training, coupled with the completely random method of selecting the instructors that caused me so much unnecessary anguish, no one in any 'executive' position seemed bright enough to realise what was going on. If they had ever stopped to really analyse the failure rate they could have saved the RAF a fortune.

"If you shout at a student every time he makes a mistake, then time the length of the tirade, then time the length of recovery that the poor victim has in which to re-engage his brain before he is able to receive more information, it comes to a total of many minutes in the flight time for each lesson. Given that the Jet Provost cost some several hundred pounds an hour to run, the behaviour must have cost thousands for many students and even more for those where it resulted in a failure.

"The later policy where it was decided that there 'was no such thing as a bad student, only bad instructors' went some way towards an improvement. But the real answer was to select from those who were available to go to CFS, and who had the basic psychological attributes that were needed."

John Grainge:

"I really enjoyed flying the Jet Provost. The side-by-side seating was good as you could see your instructor's reactions when on dual sorties which also provided a sense of security and was confidence building. The weather at RAF Linton-on-Ouse was unpredictable, to say the least and on many occasions we had to relocate to other airfields during inclement weather. RAF Elvington provided many an hour of circuit training and many students completed their first solo there on the huge 10,000-foot runway. One time we all had to fly across to RAF Valley for a couple of weeks. This was great as many hours were spent on low-level flying around the now 'Mach Loop'.

"Several interesting incidents spring to mind. On a navigation test with Flt Lt Fisher, I elected low-to-high routing but forgot the climb-out heading to high. So I decided to fly a knife-edge turn around a small lake and whilst doing so would consult my knee chart for the heading. I lost a little height in the high 'g' turn and on return to base, having passed the test, Flt Lt Fisher advised that I had made him 's**t his pants' as my starboard tip tank only just missed the water by inches.

"The Jet Provost was a superb aircraft for ab-initio training for the jet age. It obeyed the pilot's input but could sting if you pushed it to the limit. Spinning was exciting but you had to get it right to recover safely. In max rate turns you could pull huge 'g' forces (I even knocked out 'Nobby' Grey in one turn at around 10 g). The aircraft took it no problem but it needed a huge pull-back force on the stick.

"Acceleration on take-off was not dramatic but on a touch-and-go there was a kick in the back as the engine bit into the air at around 60 to 70 knots. What was really exciting was a run in and break: full power down the runway at 500 ft then a hard pull, reduce the power and climb to 1,000 ft to join the circuit.

"It was also a nervous exercise when we were asked to wind back the canopy at 40,000 ft on a solo flight to feel the cold. Boy was it cold! The Provost was so stable and created little buffet with an open cockpit.

"The performance of the Mk 4 was very adequate for basic training but at low level, solo, on full power – now that was thrilling, and you had to really concentrate. Reading the instruments was nigh impossible with the vibration – and eyeball outside of the cockpit was paramount."

John Davy had been a member of CFS Red Pelicans display team in 1970, and possibly the only person who declined to join the Red Arrows:

"I had just retired from the CFS team and was keen to continue with formation aerobatics. In January 1971 there was the dreadful mid-air collision at Kemble and my then wife, who had been a close friend of one of the pilots involved, Johnny Haddock, said no very loudly! Sad really, as I would have been the first (and last?) helicopter pilot member of the team."

Jim Burns' RAF career was somewhat short – being 'chopped' in December 1967:

"My first flight in the JP was 26 April 1967 with Flt Lt Laycock and my last was on 6 December, in the same year, with Sqn Ldr Gathercole. When you got Gathercole you knew the game was up unless you could pull something out of the hat. Unfortunately it was a formation flight and when I nearly flew up the jet pipe of my chum's aircraft and Gathercole whipped the controls out of my hands with, 'I have control', I knew that the toys were about to be called in, never to be returned. So my total Jet Provost time was under eight months…a total career flying time of 140 hours; which included about 30 hours on the Chipmunk. I was lined up on the taxiway ready to turn on to the runway one early morning, barriers down for the traffic, waiting for my chum Keith to land his JP before I took off. Keith managed to touch down on the grass the wrong side of the road, hopped over the road and then landed. He came to a stop pretty much near the take-off spot. He got 'chopped' from flying even earlier than me and went on to become a catering officer. I really wasn't a very good pilot and people slept better in their beds without me chucking ironmongery around above their heads, so I left and went to art college."

Dudley Carvell was a QFI and member of the Linton Blades display team in 1970/1971:

"On 29 January 1971, 'Nobby' Grey and I flew over to Warton to pick up a new Mk 5. I think that it was the first for Linton. I came straight back in a Mk 4 for some reason. I landed then Nobby ran in with half the station out to see the new jet. He wound it up to maximum power and pulled up to an immaculate vertical roll. Unfortunately the Mk 5 was a little lighter in pitch and he managed to pull 6.5 g. Overstressed! Jet broken! It was in the hangar for two or three days. A very embarrassed Nobby.

"I do recall that the flying was quite hard at Linton. As an example on that particular day I did five trips: a 'Blades' three-ship display in XW312 followed by the trip to Warton and back. No time for lunch because of a training sortie with 'Bradley' in XW312 for one hour ten minutes 'Intro 3', followed by a full air test in Mk 3 XM465 and to the bar."

The training of the No. 2 Flying Training School's 'Viper Red' display team for the new season began in early 1966, and during an early practice formation sortie over Woodborough, Notts, two Jet Provosts flown by Flt Lt Don Henderson (in XP631) and Flt Lt Tim Thorn and student pilot, Plt Off Mike Sedman (in XM384), were involved in a mid-air collision. All three pilots ejected safely and landed close to the wreckage. As a result of the accident, all team activities were cancelled for the rest of the year. **Air Cdre Tim Thorn** had previously suffered an engine flame-out in a Jet Provost while practising for the Wright Jubilee Trophy Competition at RAF Little Rissington in July 1965. Although he was able to land safely nothing would prepare him for the next 'incident':

"On 26 May 1966 at 0715 hours, I briefed my student, Acting Plt Off Michael Sedman, for his 19th sortie in a Jet Provost aircraft on what to expect on his first air-spinning exercise. I had been programmed to fly the 0800-hour take-off slot on that Monday morning because the aerobatic team, Viper Red, were due to practise their formation flying with the reserve pilot flying in the No. 4 position from 0730 to 0800 hours in order to maximise the training school aircraft availability and local airspace.

"Almost as soon as the aircraft entered the bright blue area, my student who was sitting on the left-hand ejection seat suddenly shouted: 'A formation is about to hit

Jet Provost Mk 3 XM384 was issued to No. 2 FTS in January 1960.

us, Sir'. Instantaneously, I pulled back the control column to raise the nose up to the vertical (this action, in the first instance, saved our lives) when there was an almighty bang and then complete silence. From the Board of Inquiry evidence later, I learnt that the Syerston team were halfway through their aerobatic sequence and had just commenced a left-hand 'card four' formation wingover when the collision occurred on the left-hand side of my aircraft. Immediately after the heavy thump, all went silent except my aircraft had now developed a high rotation spin towards the ground. On checking the 'turn and slip' indicator for the direction of the spin, I then carried out the full anti-spin actions by applying opposite rudder to the direction of the indicated spin. However, it was quite apparent that the rudders were disconnected to the pilot's control column because they moved with no apparent pressure. The aircraft was clearly in a very bad way.

"Unbeknown to me the aircraft had been cut in two just behind the cockpit by the starboard wing of the formation leader positioned at the right front of the 'card four' formation. The next moment I shouted to my student to eject, but he just looked across at me since the intercom had been lost due to the battery being chopped away with the rest of the aircraft. Subsequently, I learned that the student was asking 'Shall I eject Sir?' That said, I next moved my hands off the throttle and control column to rip my mask off when the student, who thought I was going for my ejection seat 'top' handle, decided enough was enough and he went for the bottom ejector seat handle only to leave me in a blinding flash with clouds of smoke and dust as his ejector cartridges exploded lifting the seat clear of the aircraft.

"The ejector seat was fired by powerful cartridges before rising up a tube rail. It is recorded that the student left the aircraft at 4,000 ft and in turn, I eventually exited in a similar fashion at 1,000 ft. The impact of my aircraft had resulted in the leader's aircraft bursting into flames and losing all flying control. The force of the impact moved the leader's aircraft to the left to collide with the aircraft line abreast. The leader ejected almost immediately and safely parachuted down to earth. Meanwhile, the aircraft in line-abreast position with the leader was damaged by the collision but the pilot managed to land it safely back at RAF Syerston along with the No. 4 aircraft that had been in the line-astern position on the leader. Both these aircraft were literally stripped of their paintwork by the 'fireball' which they flew through and instead of being painted in Day-Glo red they were a clean shade of metallic silver. One of the aircraft that returned to base transmitted an emergency call and alerted the rescue services.

"My aircraft – what was left after separation from the formation leader's aircraft – spiralled down to earth with bits scattering the sky. At about this time, 0810 hours or so, a man who was about to go to work had just walked down his small garden path to his garden shed to collect his bicycle before cycling to work. However, one of his bicycle tyres was flat and so he returned to the house to collect his bicycle pump which he had left on the kitchen window sill. As he re-

The wreckage of XM384 following the mid-air collision with another aircraft from No. 2 FTS's Viper Red display team over Woodborough, Notts. (Tim Thorn)

appeared through the back door and started to make his way towards the shed there was an almighty WHOOMPH.

"While the ejection was quite violent, it all happened fairly quickly and I was soon hanging from my parachute looking down to see where I was likely to land. To my horror, I could see that the wind strength was high and I was being blown towards the centre of a small village close to the city of Nottingham. All too soon the final hundred feet of the flight arrived and I was destined for either a playing field with electric cables strung across it, surrounded by spiked green-coloured palings, or a main road just before the playing field, or even worse, a large V-shaped roof. I landed into the latter, a pub called the Four Bells. I landed and disappeared into the side of the roof which removed most of my flying suit and skin. Indeed, my skin looked as if I had just been scrubbed with sandpaper; the top layer was a mass of rivulets of blood. I literally fell to the ground just short of the road, where a car was travelling left to right on the far side of the road. As with any bed sheet in a strong wind, the parachute completely enveloped the car and appeared to encompass it like a magnet. On landing, I picked myself up and surprisingly felt no broken bones or serious pain.

"Meanwhile, downwind from the car appeared this 'aberration' on the road. My student, still with his fully inflated parachute strapped to his upper body was being dragged backwards at the same time falling to the ground as the parachute dragged him off his feet. During this period the publican came out of the Four Bells pub with a bottle of whisky and some glasses. Having assisted my student to release his parachute it became very clear that he was suffering severe back pain (this is quite normal after a cartridge-fired ejection). I then managed to drag him to the butcher's shop, next to the pub where the butcher literally laid him on the 'meat slab' until collected by the ambulance. A mile away from the crash sites, the local borstal training centre for juveniles below the age of 18 years old had four of its inmates abscond while the confusion rained down over the premises. I believe they were caught two days later.

"I was taken to RAF Hospital Nocton Hall, together with my student and the leader of the formation team, where I laid on my back for four weeks due to compression of four lumbar backbones. On release from Nocton Hall I was transferred to the rehabilitation centre at RAF Headley Court. After six months of not being medically allowed to sit on ejector seats, I was cleared fit to fly again in jet aircraft. My student was also cleared after seven months. He was transferred to another course that had reached the same level as he had prior to his ejection. I did send him solo again after having flown four sorties only together. On passing the course and gaining his wings he went on to fly aircraft with two or four engines.

"The Board of Inquiry considered all the findings of our 'mid-air' collision and stated that it had been the formation leader's responsibility to remain within visual flight rules (VFR) from cloud. Further, as a pilot who operated from RAF Syerston, the leader should not have led the formation."

Mike Sedman provides a little more on the aftermath of the mid-air collision:

"I was off flying for five months following the accident in May 1966 and returned for my first flight again with Tim on 26 October. He remained my instructor until January when I was transferred to a variety of instructors until I settled down with a Fg Off Turner. I returned to the same squadron when I went back to flying duties, but that was at Syerston."

Following an operational tour in Germany flying the Canberra and a QFI course at Little Rissington, **Norman Gill** became a Jet Provost instructor with No. 6 FTS in November 1964:

"Some of my students at RAF Acklington were from Jordan and Malaya and, on 1 May 1967, I was doing circuits and bumps with a Malaysian student in Jet Provost, XM453. On lowering the undercarriage, we got red and black main undercarriage lights with a green nosewheel indication. I managed to persuade my student to refrain from ejecting and we climbed to 2,000 ft, where we circled, checked the quick ref handbook (QRH) and recycled the undercarriage.

"Then I noticed three staff cars with the CO, wing commander flying and engineering rushing across the airfield to the tower. Several flypasts were requested and I realised that the Board had been convened. Great! – all I needed to do was to follow their recommendation and I was home free. Remarkably quickly I was ordered to burn off fuel to minimum and land wheels-up on Runway 02 (not the main runway).

"Whilst orbiting my student had calmed down and requested to do the landing – I promised he could do it next time. Then we saw flashing blue lights converging on the airfield from all points of the compass. I found out later that the duty instructor had phoned the local fire brigade to request domestic cover as our own firemen stood by for a crash in 40 minutes. The word spread like wildfire round all the

RANDOM JET PROVOST MEMORIES

'Don't forget your undercarriage like this stupid pilot!' Jet Provost Mk 3 XM453 of No. 6 FTS at RAF Acklington in May 1967. (via Norman Gill)

nearby fire stations. When I landed, there were ten fire engines lined up on the other runway determined to see the spectacle and, probably, for the part-time firemen to get a call-out fee.

"The SAR helicopter arrived as we jumped out, whisking us off to sick quarters, which was uninhabited since the entire staff were in an ambulance lined up for the show. Eventually, the medical officer showed up and gave us a brandy laced with coffee – for medicinal purposes.

"It turned out that there was only one hydraulic jack for the undercarriage which worked the nosewheel directly and a master pulley drum that links it to the main legs by a leather belt which had been improperly secured and became loose. The landing was incredibly smooth with the ground effect from the low wings forming a cushion. First you hear the aerials scraping on the ground then a louder grinding noise from the fuselage then silence. Fortunately the belly was patched up and the aircraft was back on line in a few weeks.

"My next posting was to No. 3 FTS, RAF Leeming, in March 1968. Walking into the line office to sign the Form 700 on my first flight, I was greeted with a large poster showing a photo with the text: 'Don't forget your undercarriage like this stupid pilot!'"

Ian Halwood: RAFC Cranwell, 1983–1984:

"Best time of my life. I joined as a GD (pilot) 8 May 1983, and then 46 Course, RAFC Cranwell on 17 October 1983. I was one of four trainee pilots based at the

RAF College who were still awaiting that much desired solo flight, but due to the weather it just wasn't happening. After the QFIs made a quick decision to do a 'trip for a week' to BAe Warton in Lancashire, we kitted up and flew a four-ship formation to Warton on 14 March 1984. Throughout that week we completed various sorties leading up to solo (including some interesting 'dogfighting' with a Chinagraph sight drawn on the canopy). We also visited the various BAe sections including the 'new bubble simulator' and a full-size mock-up of the Typhoon.

"There was only Friday left to complete all our solos and I was the only trainee yet to complete. My instructor smiled, waved and went to the tower to observe if I needed assistance if I cocked up or had a minor issue. Every pilot remembers their first solo and mine was a delight, I felt invincible. However that invincibility was put to the test as I approached finals far too high. I remembered the brief, 'If anything lights up, just point it at the nearest school and eject'. I landed halfway down the rather large runway and taxied back into the apron to join my fellow air warriors.

"Imagine my confusion as, for some reason, BAe made a big fuss over it and the local press, assorted personnel and a company chief pilot by the name of Jeremy Lee were waiting to shake my hand and congratulate me on the solo. There was a press photo taken with him and I can't recall what Jeremy said as I was trying not to laugh and spoil the picture. We returned to Cranwell on the 16th (straight after my solo flight). I chose to stream helicopters and went to Shawbury in September 1984. Sadly, I was told to voluntarily withdraw by my assessment officer on 5 February 1985, but would be able to go back to fast jet/twin crew or multi-engine. I put the letter in (and was seen by the SMO who certified I was sane) and was sent to OASC Biggin Hill, where I was suitably informed that with no doubt my flying career was over because I voluntarily withdrew. Ironically I ended up in the Fighter Control branch and in 1987 was on a test team at Saxa Vord when I met my old Gazelle squadron commander, Rob Carter, and during a drink he explained that if I had gone via the various reviews i.e., squadron, wing and group captain, even if I failed I would have got fixed wing on multi-engines. I left the RAF in 1991 as a flight lieutenant deputy flight commander of 'E' Flight, 85 Squadron, equipped with the Bloodhound missile and based at RAF Wattisham."

Anonymous Pilot:

"'That's the only tricky thing about these aircraft,' said one of my instructors, rubbing his shin ruefully and pointing to the cockpit ladder he had just fallen off. 'Why did they have to make them so high off the ground? You need oxygen to get into the cockpit. And apart from the difficulty of climbing in and out of the thing,' he went on 'A chap trained on this aircraft should find the Vampire a piece of cake.... even if he leaves here with a dent in his shin from the ladder,' he added finally, as he hobbled off towards the flight office."

Unnamed Jet Provost student, No. 2 FTS RAF Hullavington, August 1957

"I learnt to fly on the 3s and 4s at 'Fawlty Towers' (i.e. RAFC Cranwell) in the mid-1960s; you went through to the first solo on one mark and then converted to the other. Essentially, the Mk 3s, being relatively underpowered were used for low-fatigue sorties such as IF and high-level navigation, whilst the much 'pokier' Mk 4s were used for general handling (GH) and low-level navigation exercises, hence the much higher fatigue consumption. The Mk 3s were usually flown with half tips whilst the Mk 4s were flown with full tips because of the higher fuel consumption. I also recall that two QFIs at 'Fawlty Towers' flew past the chief instructor's office, canopy wound back, lots of bank and top rudder, waving two fingers. After all, he was out of the office, wasn't he? – no, he'd just got back in! Lots of extra duties for that."

THE MAN WHO FELL TO EARTH

Jet Provost T Mk 3A G-BVEG/XN629 was sold to its new owner in March 1994. As the pilot had no previous experience of military flying, he was given flight training from a qualified instructor before taking delivery of his aircraft. This included aerobatics and procedures for abandoning the aircraft in an emergency. The right-hand ejection seat had not been properly secured during a previous maintenance service, but he was not shown how to check it as he believed it to be 'inert'.

On 3 April 1994 he decided to fly the aircraft from North Weald with his brother as a passenger on a short familiarisation trip over East Anglia. Being aware of his brother's inexperience in jet aircraft, the pilot briefed him on the procedure of abandoning the aircraft in an emergency. Flying at 3,000 feet near Colchester, the pilot began a series of aileron rolls. During the second roll the passenger felt his seat move, which then suddenly slid up the rails due to the effects of negative 'g', breaking the canopy as it left the aircraft.

As the passenger had failed to strap himself into the parachute correctly he fell free of the seat and, although not hurt, he pulled the parachute ripcord handle, which then fully opened. Despite suspended by the neck by the seat straps, he remained conscious throughout his descent and was helped by two people on the ground and the emergency services, who took him to hospital suffering with a strained neck and a swollen throat and tongue caused by the harness of the seat's quick release box.

The pilot orbited the area searching for his brother and eventually transmitted a Mayday message, as his vision had become restricted by the large hole in the canopy and he found difficulty in finding the airfield. Shortly afterwards he received assistance from a friend who was airborne in another aircraft, which he subsequently followed and made a safe landing at North Weald.

CHAPTER SIX

FOREIGN SALES

The operational equipment installed in the Jet Provost was roughly equivalent to that carried by its piston-engine predecessor, and at customer request it could be fitted with two 0.303-in machine guns fitted in the intakes and an underwing load similar to that carried by the 'Armed Provost'. As equipped, the aircraft was considered to be used for policing duties rather than for weapons training. Some nascent air arms found this concept to be attractive as they were keen to obtain the latest aircraft to achieve superiority over their rival neighbours during frequent border disputes and internal warfare.

Two armed export versions of the Jet Provost were made available, the T Mk 51 (based on the Mk 3) and the T Mk 52 (Mk 4), and despite several international

Jet Provost T Mk 51 of the Kuwait Air Force delivered to Rumaithaya Airport in January 1962. (BAe Systems Heritage Warton-Percival/Hunting Collection)

promotion tours, only a small number of contracts were eventually signed. These included 22 Jet Provost T Mk 51s: Ceylon (12), Sudan (four) and Kuwait (six), with 51 Jet Provost T Mk 52s: Iraq (20), Venezuela (15), Sudan (eight) and South Yemen (eight).

Some submissions for foreign procurements, however, were considered to be wildly impossible: in March 1961, the Congo Republic ordered ten 'Jet Provost Mk 3s' through the COGEA company in Belgium; as the Congolese air force had only been formed that same month, it came as little surprise that the sale was immediately refused by the British Foreign Office. A further order by the Greek air force for between 35 to 40 of the lightly armed version of the Jet Provost T Mk 5 trainer – the Mk 55 – was embargoed by the Labour government.

CEYLON

In December 1959, Ceylon became the first overseas country to acquire Jet Provosts with the delivery of 12 T Mk 51 aircraft for No. 10 (Jet Training) Squadron at Katunayake. Tasked with a primary role of advanced pilot training, the Jet Provosts strengthened RCyAF's ground-attack and interceptor capability and were also used for aerobatic and formation flying as part of the standard training syllabus. It was during this latter exercise that the squadron suffered its first loss the following February when a Jet Provost (CJ704) suffered an engine failure during a formation flypast rehearsal for Independence Day and crashed into the Negombo Lagoon.

Former RAF Halton apprentice, **Plt Off Noel Lokuge** became the first pilot to safely eject from a RCyAF Jet Provost:

> "We received the Jet Provost aircraft in December 1959 and I subsequently obtained a commission and graduated with my wings. I did my conversion onto the Jet Provost with a seconded RAF officer, Flt Lt Gill. At that time the RCyAF was staffed with seconded RAF officers and men, until the locals were trained. After about four hours of dual on type, Flt Lt Freddie Fielding an ex-Spitfire pilot and A1 instructor, checked me out and sent me solo.
>
> "On 1 February 1960 I was flying as No. 3 in a formation of six Jet Provosts taking part in a flypast rehearsal when I had an engine flame-out soon after take-off. I safely ejected at 350 feet and the aircraft crashed into the Negombo Lagoon. The Martin-Baker ejection seat undoubtedly saved my life."

Jet Provost T Mk 51s of No. 10 (Jet Training) Squadron, Royal Ceylon Air Force, at Katunayake soon after delivery. (RCyAF)

On 31 August 1961, the RCyAF Flying Wing was transferred to China Bay, Trincomalee, and the Jet Provosts were soon deployed in peacekeeping and deterrent roles. In January 1966, a nationwide emergency was declared because of political demonstrations and unrest caused by the newly formed Janatha Vimukthi Peramuna (JVP) 'People's Liberation Front', a small splinter group which had emerged from the Communist Party, which soon found the Jet Provosts being flown as a 'show of strength' over potential trouble spots. It was during this period that a further Jet Provost (CJ703) was lost on 17 January 1966 when it crashed into the coconut trees on approach to Katunayake Airport, killing Flt Sgt Shayir Sally.

Kris Muthukrishnan trained at RAF Halton between 1959 to 1961 before returning to Ceylon to work in the Aircraft Servicing and Modifications Flight in 1962, followed by the major repair section between 1965 to 1968:

"We had 12 Jet Provosts in our RCyAF fleet that were the armed versions. I had the task of repairing Jet Provost (CJ708) which had belly-landed c.1964/1965. I do not recollect why it belly-landed, either the landing gear system failed or the pilot forgot to lower the gear. The repair scheme came from Hunting, Luton, and we completed the major repair with a celebration party. Unfortunately, the authorities decided not to proceed with the test flight (for an unknown reason) and the aircraft never saw the sky again.

"I was also doing lots of modifications on the Jet Provosts, like covering of flight control cable pulleys etc. Similarly, I was entrusted with this modification of improving the flight canopy sealing. A new seal was installed with a retaining strap, secured with pop rivets. On completion of this mod, the aircraft went on a test flight and on return the pilot could not open the canopy, it was stuck closed. He had to jettison the canopy to get out. Investigation found that a pop rivet head had got stuck in the operating chain that had caused the problem. Reason being, break head pop rivets were used instead of break stem tucker pop rivets. Either the mod kit had the wrong rivets, or I selected the wrong ones, still a mystery until now."

By 1970, the RCyAF had placed eight of the Jet Provosts into storage at China Bay to reduce expenditure as the government did not perceive any threat that required these aircraft. But the following year No. 5 Squadron was reactivated and the Jet Provosts were returned to operational use following a further insurrection by the Marxist JVP rebels. The uprising had broken out in the form of simultaneous attacks on 5 April 1971, when several thousand insurgents attacked 74 police stations in various parts of the country. In response to the emergency, the squadron was transferred to the civil Ratmalana Airport to attack the rebel bases with rockets and machine guns. Unfortunately, on 12 April 1971, a third Jet Provost (CJ706) was lost in a fatal crash in the vicinity of Thampalakamam Bay when its engine failed whilst en route to Polonnaruwa, killing the pilot, Sgt Plt Ranjit Wijetunga.

Chira Fernando qualified as a QFI with No. 1 Flight Training School at China Bay in September 1970, where he trained cadets on the Chipmunk T.10. At the time, he was the youngest flight instructor in the RCyAF, and also kept current on helicopters whilst on duty in Mannar, preventing illegal immigration. The following is an extract from 'Tragedy over Thampalakamam' compiled by **Sqn Ldr Chira Fernando**, which is a first-hand graphic account of the accident and is included with the kind permission of the author:

"My first task following the outbreak of the JVP insurrection to establish a socialist state was on 6 April 1971, when I transported an injured policemen from Kegalle to Katunayake in a Jet Ranger. From then on, the helicopter operations were carried out non-stop from Colombo to destinations in the western, central and north central provinces, based on ground reports. The Jet Rangers were mainly used for reconnaissance flights, transporting weapons, ammunition and supplies to police stations in the island.

"The entire insurrection was considered rather primitive and disorganised, and apart from a few offensive flights in Elpitiya, Anuradhapura, Pothuhera and Kegalle, the RCyAF was fortunate that the home-made JVP weapons were crude and ineffectual. Whenever the rebels fired at the helicopters the missions become 'search and destroy'.

"On 12 April 1971, the RCyAF was heavily involved in the insurgency, and Flt Lt Manoharan and myself (as a flying officer) were detailed to drop smoke markers on a target in Polonnaruwa from a Jet Ranger helicopter. Two Jet Provosts based at Katunayake were also tasked with dropping bombs on the same target. It was early evening. The two Jet Provosts overtook our helicopter; one aircraft, flown by Flt Sgt Tudugalle was ahead and the second, flown by Sgt Plt Ranjit Wijetunga was about one mile behind him.

"I was commanding the Jet Ranger, when suddenly, it became obvious to me that Ranjit was flying slower than normal and we were overtaking him. Within minutes after we overtook him, Ranjit called up to say that he was losing power. I asked him what speed he was maintaining. There was silence. 'Check speed,' I prompted him again. '105 knots,' came the reply.

"120 knots is the best gliding speed on the Jet Provost and therefore 105 knots was far less than the best gliding speed. Both the helicopter and the Jet Provost were now over the western edge of Tampalagamam Bay and at an altitude of about 500 feet. I immediately realised that Ranjit lacked sufficient altitude; and there was no way that he could have glided to the China Bay runway. All I could do was call on the radio and shout, 'Ranjit, eject, eject! Ranjit, do you read me? Eject!' Unfortunately he did not. As we watched in horror, the aircraft nose pitched up and entered into a spin to the left. One-and-a half turns later the aircraft struck the ground at a relatively flat attitude but in a spin.

"I landed the helicopter about 30 seconds after the aircraft hit the ground and within about 50 metres of the crash site. We could see fuel pouring out of the wing root area. Fortunately there was no post-crash fire and Flt Lt Manoharan was able to reach the crashed aircraft. He then ran back shouting, 'Chira, I don't know how to make the ejection seat safe'. I had no choice but to tighten the friction on the cyclic control and jump out to assist Manoharan, leaving the helicopter unmanned and the rotors turning. Fuel was still pouring out of the broken Jet Provost's wing. The aircraft nose had sheared off to the right and Ranjit was hanging on the ejection seat straps, seemingly unconscious. His helmet was missing and so was the whole front and sides of the cockpit, where the seat safety

RCyAF Jet Provost Mk 52 CJ712 at SLAF Eagles' Lakeside Banquet & Convention Hall, Attidiya. (via Tom Singfield)

pins are stowed. Mano supported Ranjit's body while I unstrapped him. He fell into our arms. We carried him to the helicopter within a few minutes of the crash and were immediately on our way to China Bay; a mere 1NM from the crash site. I called for an ambulance and as we approached to land on the apron, I saw the ambulance speeding — away from us! I landed and shut down. We desperately shouted at the airmen using all the profanity we could muster only to find out that the ambulance had gone to pick up the doctor. We had assumed that Ranjit would survive, but the doctor confirmed that he had suffered fatal injuries. Ranjit's helmet had been flung forward off his head and his head had whiplashed back, fracturing his skull and causing his death. It was a very sombre and quiet flight as we flew his body back to AFHQ that night."

With the end of the insurgency, the RCyAF returned the Jet Provosts into long-term storage and they were finally written off in 1985 as 'unserviceable'. The survivors were preserved as gate guards or museum exhibits.

CJ701 preserved Wirawila AB; CJ702; CJ704 abandoned after engine failure, Negombo Lagoon, 1-2-60. Preserved Ratmalana; CJ705 ex-Viharamahadevi Park, Ratmalana; CJ706 (?) preserved Batticaloa AB; CJ707 Preserved China Bay; CJ709 preserved Palaly Airport, Kankesanturi (Jaffna); CJ710 gate guard, Anuradhapura AB; CJ711 Sri Lanka AF Museum, Ratmalana (marked as CJ701); CJ712 SLAF Eagles' Lakeside Banquet & Convention Hall, Attidiya; CJ705 – Viharamaha Devi Park, Colombo.

IRAQ

Between September 1964 and April 1965, the Iraqi air force took delivery of 20 Jet Provost T Mk 52s for basic and weapons training at Shaiba, with some of the flying instructors being contracted as part of the Indian Air Force training team. **AM Pattathil Venugopal** (IAF):

> "I was with the IAF training team from November 1966 to August 1969 (an extended period on request of the Iraqi air force as they held our air force in great esteem). There were no prescribed rules or regulations, and they showed immense faith and trust in us. There was always an overlap with outgoing QFIs. Our team flew the Chipmunk, Provost, Jet Provost, L-29 Delfin, MiG-15 and MiG-17Fs. This was in Basra (SHAIBA). All one did was to read the Pilots Notes and complete one trip with one of our QFIs."

Example of an Iraqi Jet Provost T Mk 52. (BAe Systems Heritage Warton-Percival/Hunting Collection)

Gp Capt Vijay Mayadev (IAF) also instructed on the Jet Provost at the Iraqi Flying Instructors School between 1974 to 1975:

> "Prior to Iraq, I had instructed on the de Havilland Vampire, T-6G Texan, HAL Kiran Mk 1 and the HAL HT-2 primary trainer with the Indian Air Force. The Jet Provost was used only at the FIS at Basra, the air force academy flew the L-29 Delfin, while the OCU operated MiG-15s. Those operated by the flying leaders school were also used for armament training.
>
> "I remember when I returned in December 1975 the Jet Provost was still their trainer. I trained about four courses of their flying instructors. There were no ground classes: general technical test, blindfold test, et al. If my memory serves me correctly, it was self-study followed by a friendly dual check and you were ready to go.
>
> "I also instructed on the MiG-15 for just about two months as a stopgap as I still had a short while before I returned home. I found the MiG-15 easy to handle though a little heavier on controls than the Jet Provost.
>
> "I am not aware of any incidents or accidents, maybe because the Iraqis insisted on having only A1 instructors at the FIS; experience and competence was not required."

Despite Gp Capt Mayadev's comment, at least four Jet Provosts were known to have been lost in flying accidents, including one that crashed to the south of Basra in February 1967.

In September 1968, the Jet Provosts were replaced by the delivery of the first batch of Aero L-29 Delfins.

NEW ZEALAND

Following the withdrawal from service of the de Havilland Vampire in December 1972, the Royal New Zealand Air Force (RNZAF) began to introduce to service the first ten of what eventually became a squadron of 16 BAC Strikemaster Mk 88 dual-seat training aircraft. The Strikemaster was widely known as the 'Blunty', and was used for the advanced stage of pilot training taking the student from the basic and intermediate stages already completed on the Harvard and CT-4B Airtrainer to wings standard on the Strikemaster. With the provision for a 7.62-mm machine gun, underwing pylon hard points to facilitate the carriage of drop tanks for extra fuel, or 'parent' racks to carry practice bombs or rocket pods, the Blunty was also a rugged and useful fighter lead-in trainer for those pilots selected to progress to the RNZAF's A-4K Skyhawk.

The first three Strikemasters were shipped to New Zealand, with NZ6361 being handed over to No. 14 (F) Squadron at Ohakea in October 1972, allowing the first course to begin the following month. An additional six Strikemasters were delivered by June 1975 to form an operations flight within the squadron to provide tactical training and weapons to students awaiting conversion to the Skyhawk.

Jim Barclay is a former RNZAF pilot who flew a number of jet fighter aircraft, including the Vampire, Strikemaster and Skyhawk, as well as the F-4 Phantom with the USAF. In his service career, he held responsibility of positions including the commanding officer of No. 14 (F) Squadron at Ohakea between February 1982 and December 1983:

> "At the time the Blunty was introduced to RNZAF service, I was flying the A-4K Skyhawk with 75 Squadron at Ohakea. After serving two years in Singapore from late 1973 until the end of 1975, I completed a flying instructor's course at RNZAF Base Wigram and became a QFI in June 1976 on the North American Harvard at the pilot training squadron (PTS), Wigram.
>
> "At PTS, student pilots were taken to a tented camp of some ten days duration at a regional airfield in New Zealand where their pilot navigation skills were advanced. On 17 November 1976, PTS deployed from Wigram to Invercargill airfield where a tented camp was set up for the duration. It was at this camp that I had my first ride in a Strikemaster, with Fg Off Peter Cross in Strikemaster NZ6363 who took me on a two-hour navex from Invercargill to Manapouri where he did a touch-and-go landing, together with Queenstown, Cromwell, Alexandra and then via Gore back to Invercargill. I remember nothing about the flight except to say I was impressed by the range of the Strikemaster, fitted with underwing drop tanks carrying extra fuel.
>
> "In January 1978 I was promoted to squadron leader and posted to Central Flying School at Wigram. One of the main roles of CFS was to train qualified RNZAF pilots to be QFIs; another task was to test QFIs for suitability to upgrade their status as an instructor.
>
> "My first solo flight in a Strikemaster was on 26 June 1978 in NZ6371 – this was 'Conv 3' that I had missed out on earlier. I completed circuits, a turn-back,

upper-air work including aeros, stalling, steep and maximum rate turns before a low-level approach to Ohakea and more circuits. I thought the Strikemaster was a 'predictable' aircraft to fly, if a little slow in rate of roll, especially early in a sortie when there was still fuel in the wingtip tanks. Throttle response was good from the Rolls-Royce Viper turbojet engine. Visibility from the roomy cockpit was also good.

"Before a posting to USA in 1979, I had one more flight in a Strikemaster, this time at Ohakea on 26 January 1979 with Sqn Ldr Peter Moore RAF in NZ6371. We did radar and mutual pursuit intercepts (PIs) and some ACM before separating from the other Strikemaster in the formation to do some aeros, and finally circuits back at Ohakea. My next Strikemaster flights would be some three years away when I was appointed as CO 14 Squadron in February 1982, having been in the USA on an exchange posting."

By the early 1980s concerns were being expressed about fatigue cracks that were discovered in the Strikemaster's tail fins and main-wing structures due to the amount of low-level operational flying being carried out by the squadron. In August 1985, further structural defects were discovered and the aircraft were temporarily grounded. Although a permanent repair was not considered to be practical, six sets of replacement wings were acquired from BAe and fitted the following year to extend the service lives of the aircraft; the 're-winged' aircraft included NZ6361, '62, '64, '69, '71 and '72 – unfortunately, the first Strikemaster that received new wings (NZ6369) crashed soon after near Reporoa during a Falcons Roost exercise based at Tauranga.

Further temporary groundings and subsequent revised course intakes resulted in a search for a replacement aircraft for the Strikemaster under the title 'Project Falcon'.

Jim Barclay again:

"Low-level turbulence was/is certainly a problem in New Zealand and undoubtedly a contributor to the shortened life of the Strikemaster. I was the project manager for Project Falcon, taking over from Gp Capt Ken Gayfer; with the team, I visited the Royal Malaysian Air Force to see their MB339s, VDO in Germany, Italian air force at Lecce and Practica di Mare, Aermacchi SPA at Venegona, Rolls-Royce, and a British company that made the wing-mounted carrier for the carriage of practice

FOREIGN SALES

BAC Strikemaster Mk 88 NZ6366 of No. 14 (F) Squadron RNZAF base Ohakea in 1989. (RNZAF)

bombs; then contract negotiations in New Zealand. The eventual acquisition of the Aermacchi MB339CB was agreed in March 1990 and the first three aircraft were handed over to the RNZAF in April 1991."

Sqn Ldr Ian 'Iggy' Wood was the CO of No. 14 (F) Squadron from December 1986–December 1987:

"After 640 hours with the Royal Singapore Air Force, I was posted to No. 14 Squadron at Ohakea as operations flight commander. The primary duty was fighter lead-in training with a secondary duty to conduct forward air controller training courses with both RNZAF pilots and NZ army personnel.

"The wing main spar attachment lug fatigue cracks (both on the wing-root ends and the carry-through centre section) had a major impact on the RNZAF Strikemaster, both on the flying and on the engineering fronts. It was of interest that the cracking was asymmetric with the upper lugs on the left and the lower lugs on the right being more damaged. This was attributed to the side-by-side seating making turning left during air combat and rolling in on ground-attack sorties more frequent as the pilot had much better visibility by doing a left turn – and often under a 5 g load.

"I cannot recall delays with the Wings Course but know that the reduced number of aircraft on the flight line made it more difficult to do the fighter lead-in training which required two, four, and occasionally six aircraft to meet the syllabus objectives. A couple of the fleet leaders in the fatigue life consumption were used for the more benign sorties of high navigation and instrument flying. We also kept a

JET PROVOST BOYS

log of individual pilot's fatigue life use so we could make sure that individuals were not over exuberant in their handling of the aircraft. Initially, a couple of pilots were found to accrue fatigue life at twice the rate of the squadron average, and we had to call for some 'guidance' to be given to ensure that the RNZAF did not run out of Strikemasters before the Macchi MB-339CB was to enter service."

With the completion of the Strikemaster's last squadron exercise, Falcons Roost 31, at Gisborne in November 1992, three aircraft, NZ6361 (Sqn Ldr M. Longstaff/Wg Cdr I. Wood), NZ6363 (Flt Lt G. Dobson/Flt Lt Wilton) and NZ6370 (Sqn Ldr B. Keightly, squadron CO) made a final flypast over the Manawatu region on 17 December 1992, following which the type was officially withdrawn from service.

Sqn Ldr 'Iggy' Wood has the final comment:

"As the wing commander of the RNZAF Flying Wing, I flew the Ohakea base commander from Ohakea to Gisborne for the Falcons Roost 31 exercise cocktail

NAF701 in Benin in 1968 with mercenary pilots Mike Thompsett (British), Charlie Vivier and Ares Klootwyk (South Africans). (Ares Klootwyk)

party on 27 November 1992 in NZ6363 and back the next day in NZ6372. My last RNZAF Strikemaster flight was in NZ6361 on 17 December 1992 as part of a three-aircraft last Strikemaster flight in RNZAF service. The RAF exchange officer Sqn Ldr Mike Longstaff was the passenger."

NIGERIA

During the 1967–1970 Biafran War, Airwork Ltd provided the Nigerian government with assistance to procure two Jet Provost T Mk 51s (143 and 157) from the Sudanese air force. The aircraft were flown from Khartoum to Makurdi in August 1967 by contract pilots, Mike Thompsett and Ralph Swift, and were allocated with the Nigerian air force serials NAF701 and NAF702. Despite poor maintenance, both aircraft were reported to have performed well in the ground-attack role while flown by the two principal mercenary pilots operating from Makurdi, Benin City and Port Harcourt. On 23 June 1969, NAF701 overshot Lagos Airport and made an emergency wheels-up landing on the edge of a lagoon near Porto Novo, Dahomey (now Benin), during a ferry flight from Port Harcourt for servicing; the two pilots, Mike Thompsett (who was later killed in July 1969 while flying a MiG-17) and Lt Dare Ralph Femi, NAF, were uninjured, and it was returned to its base by road on 5 July 1969. Although it was not confirmed as being returned to NAF for further service, the second aircraft, NAF702 remained active throughout the civil war period.

Ares Klootwyk was recruited as a mercenary pilot:

"Halfway through 1968 when the NAF were short of ground-attack pilots, I was asked if I would convert onto the Aero L-29 Delfin light-attack trainer, which they used in conjunction with the Jet Provosts. As I had started as a fixed-wing pilot in the SAAF on Harvards and Vampires, together with two years of warfare experience previously in the Congo, I said yes. Charlie Vivier converted me and I flew until November 1968, when another pilot and myself approached the NAF officer, whom we persuaded to allow us to convert from dual-control MiG-15s to single-seat MiG-17s.

"Charlie Vivier was on leave at the time but he converted later, as did Mike Thompsett in 1969. As to the Jet Provosts in the NAF, I once flew with Mike as a passenger, and he had flown a handful of missions with the MiGs and the Jet

Provost. As far as I know, only Thompsett and Swift flew the Jet Provost and I only recall them being silver/grey. I don't remember seeing a green one which is frequently mentioned. The Egyptian mechanics serviced all strike aircraft and an ex-Fleet Air Arm engineer was responsible for the helicopters, with his Nigerian air force mechanics. As soon as the Biafrans surrendered, we pilots were told that we could go home; perhaps one or two stayed on longer."

SUDAN

Following the country's independence in 1956, the newly formed Sudanese air force (SAF) was initially equipped with Provost T Mk 53 armed-training aircraft, the first of which were delivered in July 1957. Four years later, Sudan became the second overseas air arm to acquire the Jet Provost T Mk 51 when four aircraft were funded by the British government in July 1961. The order also included the facilities to provide the jet conversion of eight officers at RAF Syerston, followed by weapons training with two aircraft ('124' and '162') provided by the manufacturers.

In October 1961, the first Jet Provosts began their 3,500-mile journey to the Flying Training School at Khartoum, flown by six RAF 'volunteers' led by CFS instructor **Flt Lt David McCann:**

> "We all gathered at RAF Syerston on 5 October 1961 and undertook a couple of weeks getting ready for the ferry flight, which began on 18 October. After a rather fraught journey, we eventually arrived at Khartoum on 25 October to a 'joyous' reception as the Sudanese wanted maximum publicity for the occasion. I was later given a model of the Jet Provost I flew ('124'), which has lasted longer than the actual aircraft, which crashed a few months after I delivered it."

Following the escalation of armed rebellions and border clashes, Sudan ordered an additional eight Jet Provost Mk 52s in 1962 to equip No. 2 Fighter/Attack Squadron at Khartoum and enhance its close air support capability. The SAF later became the only air arm to be equipped with Jet Provost T Mk 55s, a lightly armed, export version of the Jet Provost Mk 5; five of which had preceded the main BAC production contract at Warton of the RAF's training aircraft and were delivered to Sudan between March and June 1969.

Flt Lt Danny Lavender was an instructor with No. 6 FTS and in January 1962 he received news of a new posting to Sudan as assistant air adviser to the Sudanese government. He completed his tour at Acklington in March, and following a short armament refresher course on the Hunter T Mk 7 at RAF Chivenor, departed to Khartoum at the end of April.

"When I landed at Khartoum in the middle of the night at the end of April 1962, there to greet me was Flt Lt Graham Poyser whom I was to replace, together with Lts Arabi and El Mahina, two of the Sudanese pilots I had trained at Ternhill. I was later introduced to Flt Lt John Sweetman who had come out to convert the pilots onto the Jet Provost and I found out that both Graham and John were both returning to the UK a week later. I was then briefed that, although I was officially an air adviser, my main role was to instruct the SAF pilots on all aspects of flying and operations. Welcomed by Lt Col Awad Khalafalla, commander of the SAF, he introduced me to many of his pilots.

"On 2 May 1962, Graham gave me a sector recce on the Provost ('103') and then John Sweetman took me up in a Jet Provost Mk 51 '124' the following day. I started instructional flying but on my fourth day, one of the Jet Provosts ('139') with two pilots on board was reported as overdue. Some news came in that there were reports of a crash some 60 miles south of Khartoum, so I went with Graham and John and we eventually found the wreckage and it was obvious that both pilots had been killed as it had caught fire. The subsequent Board of Inquiry concluded that it had accidentally hit the ground while low flying. Lt Col Awad called a meeting because he was concerned about the flying ability of some of his pilots. He was happy with those trained in the UK, and those trained in Egypt were not too bad, but the ones in Yugoslavia had never been allowed to go off solo before being sent home as fully qualified pilots. I was asked to draw up a re-training programme which was approved and I set about concentrating on flying both the Provost and Jet Provost. Gradually we introduced more advanced operational flying with battle flight formations, air-to-ground firing and dive-bombing on both types of aircraft.

"On 8 November 1962, having flown two sorties already, I was asked to do an air test on a Jet Provost Mk 51 ('157') fairly late in the morning because we wanted it on the programme next day. I climbed to 35,000 ft about 60 miles north-west of Khartoum running through the air-test schedule, and put the aircraft into a dive. Recovering after about four turns, I opened the throttle but the engine did not accelerate, remaining at idle rpm. I tried the throttle several times with no success, so I transmitted a Mayday call while looking for a place to carry out a forced landing in the desert. I put the flaps and undercarriage down, and there were two or three loud bangs before I came to rest but the undercarriage was still intact. Eventually several vehicles with soldiers, crash crews and engineers turned up, and it was decided to have a guard left and try again in the morning. It was discovered that a piece of a red plastic protective cap had blocked the fuel main nozzle, and with Col Awad as a passenger, we took off and headed back to Khartoum with the undercarriage down in case it had been damaged, and landed safely.

"A few weeks later another tragedy occurred on 3 March 1963 when the prime minister of Uganda, Milton Obote, was due to fly into Khartoum on a state visit. The Sudanese air force was instructed to escort his aircraft in and out for the visit. We decided on a formation of four Jet Provosts, with Maj Kadara in the lead because the welcoming radio conversation would be in Arabic, and I would fly in the No. 4 position and keep my visor down to hide my white face. As we passed 900 feet I had to violently try to avoid Maj Kadara's aircraft as it appeared to almost stop in the air. I guessed that he had suffered an engine failure and warned air traffic control. He glided straight ahead, obviously aiming to force land over the White Nile, about a mile beyond the airfield. I called the other two to formate on me and we intercepted the prime minister's aircraft and escorted it back to the airfield to land. I saw smoke by the bank of the Nile and told the others to land while I went to look at the crash site. The aircraft had in fact crashed on the northern bank of the Nile and I found out later that there had been no attempt to eject, probably because Kadara thought that he could make the other side. Sadly he was killed as was his passenger, an engineering air force major. We escorted Prime Minister Obote out of Khartoum three days later and I wondered whether he even knew about the tragedy.

"Things had warmed up down south in September, particularly in the winter, when the Sudanese army could not move and rebels had crossed the Ethiopia and Congo borders to raid Sudanese villages and take people and cattle back. We deployed down to Juba with the armed Provosts and Jet Provosts to defend against the rebels. I was told by the high commissioner in no uncertain terms, that I must not fire, bomb or shoot on any of these raids. I told Col Awab about my predicament but added that the high commissioner did not ban me from leading the pilots to their targets which were in difficult areas of navigation. I had to loiter while the rebels were attacked and lead them home afterwards.

"Sadly, another tragedy happened a bit later when Lt Osman, a young, lively and very capable pilot, who was authorised to do a solo general handling exercise chose to fly well *south* of Khartoum to visit his village in the desert. Eyewitnesses said later that he flew very low over the village twice and then pulled up into a loop, misjudging it and was unable to pull out of the dive. He was unfortunately killed. Flying operations continued as usual including long detachments at Juba protecting the villages in the south."

Danny Lavender's tour ended in April 1964, following which he was promoted to squadron leader and posted to CFS Little Rissington to command No. 3 (Gnat) Squadron.

SOUTH YEMEN

Prior to the withdrawal of British forces from the Aden Protectorate in November 1967, the British government set about creating the South Arabian Air Force with pilots and civilian engineers recruited by Airwork Services Ltd. Shortly before the former South Arabian Federal Government collapsed, six Douglas DC-3 transport aircraft, Augusta-Bell Sioux helicopters and DHC Beaver communication aircraft had been provided by the United Kingdom. The MoD also allocated eight ex-RAF Jet Provost T Mk 4s, which had been converted to T Mk 52 standard by Marshall's of Cambridge with the first two, '101' and '102', air freighted from Brize Norton on 12 August 1967 by a Short Belfast transport aircraft; the order being completed when the last two dismantled aircraft '105' and '108' were delivered on 31 January 1968. The attack/training squadron Jet Provosts included '101' (XS223), '102' (XS224), '103' (XS227), '104' (XS228), '105' (XP661), '106' (XR652), '107' (XP684) and '108' (XP666).

The aircraft were used in operations to assist ground forces, especially on the border with Saudi Arabia. In early 1968 a diplomatic problem arose with the Jet Provosts crossing the border and using their rockets. The British government was concerned that there would be some dispute between Saudi Arabia and the United Kingdom as contract pilots were operational with both countries, which eventually resulted in them being removed from Yemen. During the operations against the rebels in the country's mountainous region, a number of Southern Yemen air force aircraft were reported to be either lost or damaged from ground fire, including a Jet Provost which was damaged when it flew into its own rocket debris.

On 6 August 1969, the first of four Strikemaster Mk 81s (501-504) were delivered from Hurn; the order worth £1.6 million, had been originally placed in December 1966 but deliveries were delayed by precedence being given to the Saudi Arabian contract. With hostility between Yemen increasing, Saudi Arabia had threatened to cancel its multi-million defence contract if it failed to be given priority.

An arrangement was eventually achieved when Airwork pilots, Messrs Creswick and Poirrier, were 'recruited' to ferry the first two aircraft (501 and 502) from Hurn to Asmara once the initial Saudi contract had been completed; a month later, the second two (503 and 504) were ferried by the same pilots. By the time the four aircraft had been delivered, however, a new government had taken over control in the country, which was renamed the Peoples' Democratic Republic of Yemen in December 1970; the air arm becoming the Peoples' Democratic Republic of Yemen Air Force and re-equipped with Soviet-built aircraft. The maintenance contract for the aircraft had previously been awarded to Airwork Ltd, but the company was not invited to apply for the contract again and all British aircraft were subsequently sold, including four Strikemaster Mk 81s and seven Jet Provost Mk 52s, which were supplied to Singapore in March and October 1974, respectively. Despite a suggestion that at least three Jet Provost T Mk 52s had been lost during operational service in Yemen between 1968–1969, the seven aircraft sold to Singapore implies that only one of the original batch ('108') was not included in the sale.

VENEZUELA

In September 1962, an order was placed by the Venezuelan air force (FAV) for 15 Hunting Jet Provost T 52s (E-040 to E-054). The first aircraft, E-040, completed its maiden flight on 29 November 1962 and was officially handed over at Luton. All 15 aircraft were subsequently test flown before being shipped to Venezuela and reassembled at Boca del Rio airbase, Maracay, where they were test flown again by company pilot, Reg Stock, with two FAV officers as observers; the first aircraft (E-040) being flown on 27 March 1963.

Reg Stock:

> "I first entered the country on 12 February 1963. There was a large gap between the penultimate and last aircraft to be assembled and made available, so I returned to the

UK on 5 November 1963. I went back and completed the initial flight check on the last aircraft (E-054) on 18 November 1963, before leaving the country five days later."

The following is an extract from Reg Stock's logbook while testing the aircraft at Luton and in Venezuela:

At Luton (1st flight)	Test Pilot	At Maracay (all 1st flight)	2nd Pilot
E-040 29/11/62	Reg Stock	27/03/63	Lt Seguias
E-041 30/11/62	"	29/03/63	Lt Dorta
E-042 14/12/62	"	18/04/63	"
E-043	"	26/04/63	"
E-044	"	09/05/63	"
E-045	"	27/05/63	"
E-046	"	10/06/63	Lt Sequias
E-047	"	21/06/63	"
E-048	"	15/07/63	Lt Dorta
E-049	"	13/08/63	Lt Sequias
E-050	"	31/07/63	"
E-051	"	21/08/63	Solo
E-052	"	29/08/63	"
E-053	"	17/09/63	"
E-054	"	18/11/63	Lt Dorta

The first Jet Provost Mk 52 for Venezuela on an air test in November 1962. (BAC via Reg Stock)

A formation of FAV Jet Provost T Mk 52s were regularly used to promote patriotism during public and international events. (FAV)

The FAV's Jet Provosts were based at the Military Aviation School's Air Training Group at Mariscal Sucre AB, and during 1964 formed an aerobatic display team, '*Los Aguiluchos*' ('Small Eagles'), comprising four aircraft led by Capt Homero Contreras. The team's role was to demonstrate the capabilities of the FAV and promote patriotism during public and international events, and made its public debut on 15 July 1965 at the FAV's anniversary celebrations. Although succeeded by a team of four de Havilland Vampire aircraft in 1965, a further display team of four Jet Provosts, '*Los Escorpiones*' ('The Scorpions') from the Air Training Group of the Military Aviation School made its debut at the 50th anniversary celebrations of Venezuelan aviation at Miranda AB, La Carlota, Caracas, on 3 July 1970. The team comprised four instructors: Capt Fredys Arguelles, Capt Guillermo Hernandez Martinez, Lt Hector Enrique Segovia Romero and Capt Germain Antonio Rodriguez Barniz.

By 1978, the Jet Provosts had been replaced by North American T-2D Buckeyes. During the 15 years of operational service with its Jet Provosts, it was the FAV's proud claim that it had never suffered a fatal accident – despite one aircraft which was lost on 15 July 1965 when a cockpit fire forced the two pilots to eject over Lake Valencia.

In 1966, 12 of the FAV's Jet Provosts were re-numbered and although it has proved difficult to determine the respective serial tie-ups with any accuracy, the airframes included were: '3309' (ex-E-050), '4332', '4362', '4704' (ex-E-043), '4734', '5324', '5354' (ex-E-048), '5364' (ex-E-042), '6750', '6780', '9385' and '9515'. By 1990 several derelict airframes were also noted at El Libertador, Palo Negro, including '3309', '4704', '5354', '5634' and '6750', and were thought to have been subsequently scrapped. Two further airframes, '5324' and '9415', were later noted at Maracay/Mariscal Sucre, while '6780' and 'E-040' are with the Museo de la FAV, Aragua, Maracay.

CHAPTER SEVEN

THE BAC STRIKEMASTER

The BAC Type 167 was derived from the Jet Provost T Mk 5 and designed specifically for export as a light-attack aircraft. Fitted with a more powerful Viper Mk 535 (20F20) engine, its stressed wing structure featured hard points capable of carrying a variety of underwing loads up to 3,100 lbs on four pylons per wing. The options typically included four 75-gallon fuel tanks, four 500-lb bombs, 24 SURA R80 rockets, eight 25-lb practice bombs or 20-lb fragmentation bombs, four 18-tube SNEB 68-mm rockets or two 0.5-inch mini-gun pods. In addition, two 7.62-mm Fraser-Nash machine guns, with 600 rounds of ammunition were fitted in the lower intake lips. An optional G90 camera gun could also be installed in the nose cone with LFS 5, GM 2 or SFOM gunsights provided for either or both seats. A revised fuel system included conformal fuel tanks on the wingtips, each containing 48 Imp gal.

In October 1968, the BAC 167 was finally renamed as the 'Strikemaster' and two prototype aircraft, G27-8 and G27-9, were temporarily allocated for company development trials, the first of which had earlier flown in October 1967.

The first customer for the Strikemaster was Saudi Arabia which placed an initial order for 25 aircraft in May 1966, the first of which was delivered in September 1968 to serve in the training and light-attack role. Over the next ten years, a total of 150 Strikemasters were built for overseas customers at Warton, ten of which were assembled at Hurn; deliveries were finally completed in May 1978 when '1135' was officially handed over to the Royal Saudi Air Force.

With the increased production of the Jaguar tactical strike fighters at Warton, it was decided to assemble a further ten Strikemasters at Hurn against possible future sales to foreign air arms. Hurn had already manufactured the wings for the Jet Provost since 1966 and was short of work following the completion of the sub-contract to build BAC 1-11 short-range jet airliners. Therefore, in November 1979 the first Strikemaster fuselage for the newly established Hurn final assembly line was transferred from Warton and made its initial flight on 7 August 1980 as G16-26. The following month it was registered as G-BIDB for use as a company demonstration aircraft. It was joined by Hurn's second Strikemaster, G16-27/G-BIHZ, and made its first production test flight on 23 October 1980.

Despite initial optimism, sales of the Strikemasters assembled at Hurn were slow to materialise until 1983, when the Sudan government offered to purchase the complete batch. The first three aircraft (141, 142 and 144) were delivered from Hurn in November 1983, with the remaining airframes being subjected to an arms embargo following a renewed outbreak of fighting in the country. The next three Strikemasters made their maiden flight from Hurn, but with the closure of the site in May 1984 the four uncompleted aircraft were returned to Warton by road between December 1983 and January 1984. Of the seven remaining Strikemasters, one was delivered to Oman (425) in September 1986 and the remaining six were sold to Ecuador, including the last four to be delivered from Warton (FAE261–FAE264) on 21 October 1988.

Among the many sales demonstrations carried out by the two aircraft included those at the Farnborough and Paris air shows, together with displays and evaluations for various visiting foreign ministers and defence attachés. During May 1981, G-BIDB and G-BIHZ were flown to Khartoum by Reg Stock and Don Thomas to celebrate Sudan Armed Forces Day.

Lt Cdr Dave Eagles RN graduated from the ETPS in 1963 and served with the Naval Test Squadron at Boscombe Down for three years. In 1968 he was appointed as senior pilot of 809 Squadron, leading the Buccaneer aerobatic team at the Farnborough show in the same year. He joined BAC as an experimental test pilot in October 1968:

> "My first trip I had with BAC was in a Jet Provost. Thereafter I flew the 'Provost 27' (The name 'Strikemaster' doesn't appear in my logbook until the end of 1971) on production testing, and after quite a bit more of testing in 1969, I flew with Reg Stock on a delivery to Riyadh in August 1971. My only memories of those days are that I was unimpressed with the sitting position, since although not of a

The first three Jet Provost Mk 52s were delivered to the Kuwait Air Force in January 1962. (BAe Systems Heritage Warton-Percival/Hunting Collection)

notably short sitting height, I needed the seat at the top of its travel at all times; and recovery from the spin was a bit prolonged at one of the fuel states we checked — half full tips? No other comments apart from it being a good, rugged performer; you could chuck it around in both the ground-attack and the trainer role without it biting back.

"With regard to the Strikemasters appearing at the Paris and Farnborough shows: my trip to Paris on 28 May 1969 was just a delivery, with a return on 9 June, with G27-35 (G-AXEF); no aerobatics so presumably just for a static display. For the Farnborough display on 7 to 10 September 1970 I was in BAC-167 143 (G-AYHS). I had just one practice and one display on 5 June 1971 in BAC 167 G27-189 (G-AYVK) for the Paris Air Show, and in September 1972 I had G27-200 (G-AZXK) at Farnborough for the week, 4 to 9 September (The show was washed out on the 8th)."

Of the 150 Strikemaster airframes produced at Warton, nine air arms received their own variants: Saudi Arabia – Strikemaster Mk 80 and Mk 80A; South Yemen – Strikemaster Mk 81; Oman – Strikemaster Mk 82 and Strikemaster Mk 82A; Kuwait – Strikemaster Mk 83; Singapore – Strikemaster Mk 84; Kenya – Strikemaster Mk 87; New Zealand – Strikemaster Mk 88; Ecuador – Strikemaster Mk 89; Sudan – Strikemaster Mk 90; Botswana – Strikemaster Mk 83 and Mk 87.

BOTSWANA

The air arm of the Botswana Defence Force (BDF) was formed in April 1977 as a result of escalating tension and border incursions in Southern Africa. To improve its strike capability, the BDF acquired nine reconditioned Strikemaster Mk 83s/87s from BAC, where they had been held in store at Warton following previous service in Kenya and Kuwait. The first three aircraft were delivered to Francistown in April 1988.

Derick Bridge joined the RAF in 1955 as an air signaller and trained on the Anson and Prentice at RAF Swanton Morley, the Shackleton MR1 and T4 at Kinloss and a tour on the MR3 on 201 Squadron at RAF St Mawgan. In October 1962 he completed his basic flying training on the Provost at RAF Ouston, before transferring to RAF Oakington for advanced training on the Vampire Trainer. Derick later qualified as a QFI at CFS Little Rissington, and then instructed at RAF Syerston for the next three years (1964–67):

"I approached BAe and eventually was offered a job as a contract pilot-instructor with the BDF on Strikemasters, but accompanied and better paid. I had previously flown the Strikemaster in Oman (and a little in Kenya), and was employed to run the Botswana operation. I started at Warton in January 1988 and began the conversion training for two BDF instructors in February. We flew OJ1 initially until OJ2 became available, then used both until 18 March. By then, OJ3 had been completed and we set off for the ferry to Botswana, led by an HS125. I flew OJ2. The route took 13 days due to the technical issues in Morocco. We arrived at Francistown in March 1988, via Warton, Bordeaux, Tangiers, Casablanca, Agadir, Las Palmas, Nouakchott, Freetown, Libreville, Kinshasa, Mbuji-Mayi and Lusaka.

"The Botswana Strikemaster was the BDF's advanced trainer, but also the operational fighter/ground-attack aircraft and I was therefore able to instruct all the way from conversion to weapons via tactics, battle formations etc. Our Strikemasters were fitted with the normal two internal machine guns, two 20-mm podded Matra cannon and two SNEB pods. (We actually fired the lot from three aircraft for a firepower demonstration for the president in 1990.) We were also fitted with a single ALE 40 flare dispenser under the rear fuselage.

"I was in charge of the Strikemaster flying at Francistown, but I don't think anyone ever told me that. We started flying immediately, continuing the training for the two Botswana instructors, although the students didn't arrive until September. The second delivery of three aircraft (OJ5, 6 and 7) arrived in July and was followed

Strikemaster Mk 83 OJ9 of the BDF was written off when the pilot attempted to avoid a herd of antelope crossing the runway at Francistown in November 1989. (via Derick Bridge)

thereafter by OJ 4 and 9 in September, giving us our full complement of nine aircraft. A final aircraft (OJ10) was obtained from Kenya (ex-605) during 1993.

"There was a lieutenant colonel who was the base commander (the 'base' being just actually one military hangar, the rest being civilian) and he had a couple of admin clerks. There was also a captain engineer plus a bunch of ground crew who actually left for Strikemaster courses in the UK as we arrived. We had some BAe ground crew initially, then others at various times for mods etc. Later, groups of Indian Air Force SNCOs arrived and were controlled by the UK chief engineer; the UK nationals being directly recruited by the BDF. Alongside me there was the BAe rep who was consulted on any problems and was the direct link to the factory. Later, the salesman who sold the aircraft to Botswana moved into the capital, Gaborone, but although he came up frequently he didn't seem to have a function other than PR.

Until we arrived at Francistown, it only supported detached aircraft from Notwane, but nothing permanent. We used Notwane when operating in the south and when visiting HQ. We also used Selebi Phikwe as our nearest diversion and Maun, where we could refuel by having to push the aircraft to the fixed pump. I left Botswana when the contract ended in 1991."

In 1996, 13 ex-Canadian CF-116s (ten single-seater CF-5As and three trainer CF-5Bs) were ordered to replace the Strikemasters, and in April 1997, with the exception of OJ3 which became a gate guard at Thebephatshwa Airbase, the surviving aircraft were sold to Global Aviation at Binbrook, where they were refurbished for resale to the civil market.

KENYA

The Kenyan Air Force (KAF) was formed in June 1964. As part of a modernisation programme to protect the country's air space and offer air support to its ground forces, Kenya was keen to buy aircraft from Britain, signing a letter of intent with BAC in May 1969 to obtain six BAC 167 Strikemasters. The following year, President Jomo Kenyatta officially announced that the KAF had successfully acquired a batch of Strikemaster Mk 87s (601–606) to equip its first strike squadron – No. 8 Squadron, based at the Flying Training School, KAF Eastleigh.

The crew members selected for the ferrying of the first two aircraft were Sqn Ldr Terry Lloyd, a GD training instructor from RAF Leeming and ex-Canberra pilot, Flt Lt David Curry. **Terry Lloyd**:

"We flew the first two Kenyan aircraft (601 and 602) whilst at Warton, and received our conversion training by the senior production test pilot, Pete Ginger. The Strikemaster

Strikemaster Mk 87 '601' was one of the first to be delivered to Eastleigh Airport, Nairobi for the Kenyan Air Force by Terry Lloyd in February 1971. (BAe Systems Heritage Warton-Percival/Hunting Collection)

avionics included VOR/DME, ILS, radio compass and HF radio, and we needed to have practice using them as we had not flown in any of the airway routes, or used the aids previously, so we had a steep learning curve. We flew one airways trip with Pete and then David and I flew mutual flights using all the aids. We made our first flight on 18 December 1972 and had a further three flights before Christmas followed by three more flights before our departure on 5 January 1971. It was quite an adventure but we finally arrived safely at Eastleigh on 12 January 1971."

On 4 July 1970, Terry Lloyd assumed the post of OC flying at KAF Eastleigh; his specification being to command the flying wing, which comprised a transport wing equipped with four DHC-4 Caribou, and three DHC-2 Beaver, together with six DHC-1 Chipmunk aircraft for training purposes. His remit also specified the introduction of the Strikemaster to the KAF and in the longer term acting as air adviser with a handover of the OC flying appointment to a Kenyan officer, Maj Dedan Kichuru in mid-1971.

Prior to the introduction of the Strikemaster, the training of Kenyan pilots had been undertaken by RAF Loan Service officers at KAF Eastleigh, with the Chipmunk for basic training and the Beaver for the advanced phase; at this stage the students were awarded their brevets and transferred to either the Beaver or Caribou squadrons. As there were no jet aircraft in the KAF, Maj Larry Mwanzia (the designate 8 Squadron commander), was detached to RAF Leeming for jet conversion in preparation for the Strikemaster deliveries, with Lt Joshi transferring to the CFS for QFI training; five other officers were sent to the RAF College, Cranwell.

On 16 February 1970, the second pair of aircraft, KAF 603 and KAF 604, arrived, while the final two aircraft KAF 605 and KAF 606 arrived on 1 April, with the squadron commander, Maj Mwanzia on board, being the only African pilot involved in the ferry flights from the UK.

Joe Whitfield:

"In mid 1970 I was selected to be part of a team of two to train the Kenyan Air Force pilots on the Strikemaster. The other pilot was Flt Lt Dave Curry, ex-Canberras and also one of the pilots who flew Spitfires during the making of the film 'The Battle of Britain'. We both arrived in October 1970 to await the completion of the Strikemasters at Warton.

"I was due to collect and deliver one of the first two aircraft, 601 and 602, but dental problems caused me to miss out. I did, however, take part in the ferrying of one of the second two aircraft, 603 and 604. After post-production air tests at Warton we set off for Kenya on 9 February 1971. Even though we had drop and tiptanks the legs were fairly short. The routing took us via Thorney Island, Nice, Brindisi, Athens, Akrotiri, Diyarbakir (Iran), Tehran, Kuwait, Bahrain, Riyadh, and Jeddah, where we were arrested because the Kenyans had not applied for the overflight of Saudi Arabia and the landing rights. Fortunately, the RAF Air Attaché happened to be there and after pulling some strings we were allowed out. Onwards via Asmara, Hara Meda and the Eastleigh base.

"The third pair of aircraft, 605 and 606, departed Warton on 19 March. I was leading in 606 with the squadron commander, Maj Larry Mwanzia in the right-hand seat. Sqn Ldr Bill Jago, the air ops man from the KAF Headquarters was my No. 2 in 605. Same routing, but when we got to Bahrain on 22 March, the Saudis would not let us into their air space as the Kenyans had cocked up the diplomatic clearance again. We spent a week in Bahrain while that was sorted out and eventually flew on to Riyadh on 31 March."

The KAF's Strikemasters successfully carried out their first range training with guns in Samburu during March 1971. This was followed by Madaraka Day on 1 June 1971, when all six of the aircraft took part in their first national day flypast at Uhuru Park in the presence of President Jomo Kenyatta; this was the first time following independence that jet fighters had taken part in a national day flypast and were enthusiastically greeted by cheers from the crowd. The jets then returned for separate barrel rolls low over the crowd before climbing and returning to Eastleigh.

On 22 June 1974 the Strike Squadron moved to the newly completed Laikipia Airbase and were joined by the KAF's first fully combat jet fighter, the Hawker Hunter, five days later. The first three Hunters of the then Air Defence Squadron (later re-named No. 11 Tactical Fighter Wing) were escorted by the Strikemasters as they arrived.

The following month the squadron suffered its first fatal accident when Strikemaster KAF 603 crashed in Meru on 22 July, with the loss of Lt Mwirigi. This was followed on 5 July 1985, by KAF 606, which made an emergency landing in Isiolo while flown by a student pilot, Lt P.K. Mwangi; he fortunately survived, but the aircraft was completely written off. It was subsequently recovered and relegated as a gate guardian at Laikipia Airbase.

The last two Strikemaster Mk 87s (KAF 605 and KAF 606) destined for the Kenyan Air Force were temporarily held at Bahrain for diplomatic clearance in March 1971. (KAF)

With the delivery of the BAe Hawk Mk 52s to No. 11 Squadron (Tactical Fighter Wing) in 1970, the Strikemasters supplemented the Hawks in the jet training and ground-attack role until the Strike Squadron was disbanded. The four surviving aircraft KAF 601, 602, 604 and 605 were returned to BAe Warton in 1986 and eventually resold to Botswana.

Two of the former Kenyan aircraft later became subject of a dubious sale to the Ivory Coast in February 2003:

KAF 601 (ex-Botswana OJ4) was registered in the UK as G-AYHR in April 1997 and changed to G-UNNY in March 1998. It was sold to Strikemaster Films Ltd, London & Ivory Coast during February 2003 as TU-VRA and last noted as being withdrawn at Abidjan in August 2015.

KAF 602 (ex-Botswana OJ5) registered in the UK as G-BXFP in April 1997 and noted in RNZAF markings. It was also sold to Strikemaster Films Ltd, London & Ivory Coast in February 2003 as TU-VRB and flown as far as Malta, where it was impounded. With the legal problems being eventually resolved, it continued on to Algiers the following month and operated with the Force Aérienne de la Cote d'Ivoire as TU-VRB. Its registration was cancelled in October 2004 and the Strikemaster was last noted at Abidjan in August 2015.

SAUDI ARABIA

In May 1966, Saudi Arabia became the first customer for the Strikemaster when it placed an order for 25 aircraft as part of a complete air-defence-system package worth £118 million. The delivery of the initial order of 12 Strikemaster Mk 80s began on 26 August 1968 with three aircraft ('903', '904' and '905'), followed by the first batch of upgraded Mk 80As (1101–1113) in 1973. With further orders to provide for the expansion of RSAF and as attrition replacements, the contracts for 146 aircraft were finally completed in May 1978.

Pilot training courses at the King Faisal Air Academy (KFAA) at Riyadh – the equivalent of the RAF College at Cranwell – included 12 months on English language and academic courses, following which the Saudi students underwent flying grading with ten hours on the Cessna 172. With the primary flying training and wings stage on the Strikemaster, the students then progressed to front-line aircraft.

The majority of the original flying instructors at the KFAA were ex-RAF. Former Hunter pilot and QFI, **Don McClen** had been initially recruited as chief instructor at the KFAA, but his appointment was changed to head of flying training and planning shortly after his arrival at Riyadh:

> "The initial contract for 25 Strikemasters in 1966 had been part of a significant government order which included 40 Lightnings. In 1972, the Saudi government ordered ten more Strikemaster Mk 80As, and the original 25 were modified to the same standard including the ability to carry guns and a light bomb load. This was followed in 1976 by 11 more aircraft to provide an expansion of the RSAF and compensate for a few Strikemasters lost in accidents. The original requirement called for 65 per cent of the aircraft to be fully available for flying duties at the start of the day.
>
> "When I first arrived in Saudi in 1975 there was a BAC weapons training instructor at the KFAA doing nothing apart from twiddling his thumbs but, by the end of the year, he had been retrained as a Link trainer instructor. To my knowledge, and that of the CFI who was there from 1975 to at least 1982, there never had been any live weapons training at any stage during a course – and no weapons squadron."

Steve Stanton was a former Cranwell flight cadet and QFI, and employed as a Pilatus PC-9 instructor between July 1988 and November 1996:

"The PC-9s had arrived in Saudi during 1988 with the first student course starting during that summer. In November 1988, the PC-9 fleet was grounded following a structural issue and to keep the training pipeline going we ex-Jet Provost instructors were swiftly shuffled, with our students, across to the Strikemaster. As it turned out we only spent a month and a half on this aircraft before we were back on the PC-9, and my last flight in the Strikemaster was on 15 January 1989.

"At first, the basic course (previously pure Strikemaster) was split into two modules; the first module was flown on the PC-9 leading on to the Strikemaster. This was never the long-term plan and, as more PC-9s arrived and the Strikemasters began to run out of fatigue hours, in 1991 we switched to two 'parallel' but identical PC-9 and Strikemaster courses, with the majority of students training on the PC-9.

"In the early years the RAF effectively ran the school. Col Shokair (RAF trained) commanded the unit until 1992, when it was handed over to Col Othman (American trained); the flight commanders, squadron commanders and wing executives, including the CFI were all company men and ex- or serving RAF officers. By the time I arrived, the King Faisal Air Academy had been pretty much 'Saudi-ised' with the squadrons commanded by Saudi officers and young Saudi instructor pilots taking on junior roles. This was an enormous cultural change for the old-timers."

Erik Mann left the RAF after some 26 years as a pilot. His last tour was as the deputy chief instructor at RAF Church Fenton in Yorkshire, where he flew the Jet Provost and Tucano T1. At this point he had some 6,727 hours total with about 1,690 of those on the various marks of Jet Provost:

"I joined British Aerospace on the Al Yamama project as an A2 QFI on the Strikemaster, arriving in Saudi Arabia in early 1991 just after the Gulf War with the oil fires still burning in Kuwait and the whole of Riyadh covered in a thin film of oil which made all the cars look very shiny until the sand dust-coated them again. The KFAA base was to the north of the city but a suburban development was gradually surrounding the airfield which is now known as the King Salman Airbase.

"I started conversion training on 20 May 1991 with a local familiarisation sortie captained by the KFAA commandant, Brig Gen Shokair and continued with BAe standards staff for six conversion trips, then a company acceptance check and finally a RSAF acceptance check with Sqn Ldr Masroor of the Pakistani air force (on secondment). Two instrument sorties then an instrument rating followed and finally a formation lead check to complete my arrival.

"Instructional sorties lasted just over an hour and were flown in a 'box' allocated for the trip by operations. This box system was based on that used in the USA, although the flying syllabus just about followed the RAF basic flying training syllabus. As there was a large USAF detachment at Riyadh our circuit training was limited to the base, with the old airfield at Al Kharj extensively used instead. The main runway at KFAA was about 13,000 ft long but we were not allowed to use the cross runway as it was only about 11,000 ft long and the circuit pattern went close to a couple of sensitive areas, one of which was a royal palace, I believe.

"Another problem in the extreme heat was that there were only a limited number of sunshades for the aircraft, and they tended to leave some BAC 167s out in the relentless sun. Our working day was two shifts starting early to avoid the heat and a changeover at lunch time. If you were on the late shift and were allocated an aircraft that had baked in the sun all morning it was very easy to burn yourself on the metal buckles of the seat harness when strapping in, especially as everyone only wore a thin undergarment and a flying suit. Sweat loss was a problem and when you got home after a couple of trips the back of your flying suit was a patchy circle of salt crystals that you had sweated out during the day. Some of the low-level navigation routes covered large featureless desert where often the best fix was a change in the colour of the sand or the texture of the terrain from red sand hills to rocky desert. In the summer the turbulence was very tiring as was the heat under the large Perspex cockpit.

"The staff on the squadron were mainly old-Commonwealth QFIs from the UK, Australia, New Zealand, Canada and South Africa, but the squadron commander was an RSAF major and about five of the QFIs were also RSAF. One of these was a Mutawa (religious police) who kept an eye on both the RSAF staff and students and the BAe personnel. The job security was limited as any slight offence to the RSAF personnel could result in a window seat back home with little or no recourse, however, most QFIs realised this early on and played to the local rules to keep their jobs.

"One unusual event was the 25th anniversary of the KFAA on 24 September 1994 when a large air display was organised and some senior members of the Saudi royal family attended. The Strikemasters were required to fly a formation in the shape of an Arabic 'F' for Faisal. The formation would be viewed from the front so we had to fly directly towards the main spectator dais at 90 degrees to the display line. The formation shape was a challenge as the Arabic letter was a dot above a vertical line then from the bottom of the line an upward slant. If I remember correctly, we used about 12 aircraft to make the shape and some of the positions required the pilots to fly formation on references that were behind them. On the day all went well and we were followed in to open the show by a PC-9 formation. After the initial flypast we picked up a couple of more Strikeys and formed four boxes of four and the PC-9s did likewise. The whole lot of us held over the city at about 1,000 ft then flew back to make a pass along the display line in mass formation.

"In November 1996 the RSAF decided (with little or no warning) to stop training on the Strikemaster. I was by now the Strikemaster fleet manager and when I arrived at work after a weekend it was a shock to find that I and all my QFIs were out of a job. After a long session with the senior BAe manager, the selected QFIs who remained had enough time left on their contract to convert to the PC-9, while the rest of us left to return to our home countries. I later advised the RAF on the setting up of a contract for employment of retired RAF QFIs as civil servant aviation officers back in the UK and so landed myself a job flying the Tucano at RAF Linton-on-Ouse for the last ten years of my flying career."

Following the RSAF's replacement with the turboprop Pilatus PC-9, the last Strikemaster flight was flown on 4 January 1997.

SINGAPORE

In July 1968, 16 Strikemaster Mk 84s were ordered on behalf of the Singapore Air Defence Command (SADC), the first of which were delivered the following October and initially issued to No. 1 Flying Training Squadron at Tengah for advanced pilot training. Formed in August 1970, the unit was one of two component squadrons of No. 130 (Eagle) Squadron; the other squadron being No. 150 (Falcon) Squadron, operating Cessna 172Ks.

With further Strikemaster deliveries to the squadron, the first local training course began in January 1970 with a mixture of loan service and contract instructors, thereby enabling the SADC to train its students up to wings standard at Tengah, rather than overseas. Four Singaporean pilots initially received flying training in the UK, who returned immediately to join 130 Squadron at Tengah; whereas one pilot, Capt Gary Yeo, proceeded to the CFS, Little Rissington, for training as an instructor and returned in April 1971 to join 130 Squadron as the first Singaporean QFI. The first eight cadets to receive their training on Strikemasters graduated on 27 November 1970.

On 15 September 1971, the RAF handed over Tengah to the SADC, which then was renamed as Tengah Airbase. However, as a result of increased fighter operations at the base, the flying training school and its two squadrons moved once again to Changi Airbase in February 1972.

To augment the Strikemaster fleet two further purchases were made in 1974, including four Strikemaster Mk 81s and seven Jet Provost T Mk 52s from South Yemen. The four Strikemasters – 320:W (ex-'501'), 321:X (ex-'502'), 322:Y (ex-'503') and 323:Z (ex-'504') – were flown to Changi Airbase during March and June 1974. These were joined by the seven Jet Provost T Mk 52s – 350 (ex-'101'), 351 (ex-'102'), 352 (ex-'104'), 353 (ex-'105'), 354 (ex-'106'), 355 (ex-'107') and 356 (ex-'108') – which were shipped to Singapore by the Republic of Singapore Navy, the following October. Following refurbishment, the first aircraft took to the air in December 1975, but with the significant differences between the Strikemasters and the Jet Provosts, the latter were not used to support the cadet training courses but instead were primarily operated for the flight instructor courses.

On 1 April 1975, the SADC was renamed the Republic of Singapore Air Force (RSAF), and due to its rapid expansion programme, five additional Strikemaster Mk 82s – 327 (ex-'402'), 328 (ex-'404'), 329 (ex-'407'), 330 (ex-'408') and 331(ex-'409') – were purchased from Oman, arriving at Changi Airbase in May 1977. However, the Jet Provosts were withdrawn in 1981 when it became increasingly difficult to continue operating the aircraft due to the lack of spares and high maintenance costs.

Bruce Byron RAAF was loaned to the RSAF from June 1976 to December 1979 as OC Standards Squadron:

> "My task was to set up a CFS-type system where we ran flying instructor courses and examined the QFIs on operational types – the A-4 Skyhawk, Hunter, Skyvan, C-130 and Alouette choppers. I was assisted by another RAAF QFI and we gradually introduced RSAF QFIs into the standards role, which was handed over to local the QFIs when I left.
>
> "The Strikemasters were employed for the advanced phase of the pilots' course, while the SF-260s were used for the basic phase. All trainee QFIs were trained by Standards Squadron on four Jet Provost Mk 52s that were procured by the RSAF just before I arrived. We used a RAAF/CFS 100-hour training syllabus, which of course was similar to the RAF CFS course.
>
> "During my time, the Jet Provosts were used exclusively for the flying instructor courses run by the Standards Squadron. From my arrival in July 1976 to early

1978 the only airframes online for our use were '350', '351', '352' and '354'. From January 1978, '356' also came online and was there until I left in December 1978, while '355' came on line in April 1978. About two weeks after I arrived in July 1976 a student on No. 1 Flying Instructors Course ejected from one of the Jet Provosts ('351') on his first solo on type. He claimed he couldn't recover from a spin – which was very unusual in a JP3/4.

"The RSAF wanted a Strikemaster display pair and it was appropriate that it be flown by local pilots – not Aussies or others. With my Red Pelicans and Roulettes background I trained both pairs during 1976 and 1977. In 1976 it was Lt Ng (lead) and Lt Foo Hee Tim. In 1977 Lt Fernandez (lead) and Capt Mickey Liew. I trained each pilot for low-level synchronised aerobatics progressively clearing them at 3,000 ft, down to 1,500 ft, 1,000 ft and finally at 500 ft AGL. Then we put the display together. All displays and practices were done over Changi Airbase so the pair could use the main runway (either side) for lateral separation during the numerous head-on passes."

Sqn Ldr 'Iggy' Wood:

"I was 'on loan' to the Republic of Singapore Air Force from January 1977 to October 1978 – 'loan' means that there was not an exchange person from the RSAF to the RNZAF. I had a total of six hours in the Strikemaster at Ohakea in December 1976 before travelling to Singapore. All of my flying instructor hours to date were on Harvards and Devons. After 14 hours with the RSAF Standards Squadron, I was let loose as a line instructor with No. 130 Squadron. No. 130 Squadron was based at Changi, which was undergoing construction to become Changi International Airport. The RSAF had an initial buy of 16 Mk 84 Strikemasters. These were the first Strikemasters which I saw while in Singapore doing a month-long duty as an operations officer for RNZAF No. 14 Squadron on the Canberra swansong in June 1970; Exercise Bersatu Padu, I think. When I arrived at Changi in 1977, the RSAF had three out of the four Mk 81 ex-Yemen Strikemasters ('320' to '323') extant and a number of the Jet Provost Mk 52s. I had only one ride in a Mk 52 '352' as the RSAF used those for their flying instructor courses. The RSAF ferried five ex-Omani Mk 82 ('327' to '321') from the Middle East to Changi: my first flight in a Mk 82 was in September 1977. Although the RSAF did not lose any Strikemasters during my time, there were a couple of minor events; the Strikemasters involved were repaired promptly and back on the flight line."

With the development of Changi as Singapore's new international airport, the FTS and its units was relocated to Paya Lebar Airport in July 1981. No. 130 Squadron continued to operate the Strikemasters until 1986, when they were finally withdrawn and replaced by the SIAI-Marchetti S.211 advanced jet trainer.

During 17 years of operations with the SADC, eight Strikemasters and one Jet Provost were written off in flying accidents. The most poignant loss was that of Capt Michael Teo and a student in a SF-260 light combat aircraft during January 1981; seven years earlier, Capt Teo had survived an ejection from a Strikemaster which had crashed into the sea off Changi AB. The losses included:

Jet Provost Mk 4 '351' (ex-XS224 and South Yemen AF 102); control lost and crashed into sea near Tengah, 13-8-76.
Strikemaster Mk 81 '320' (ex-South Yemen 501); crashed near Labis, Jahore (2) 13-6-75.
Strikemaster Mk 81 '321' (ex-South Yemen 502); crashed 3-12-80.
Strikemaster Mk 84 '300'; engine failed on approach, Tengah (1K 1 injured) 28-1-76.
Strikemaster Mk 84 '303'; engine failure; pilot ejected over South China Sea, 7-5-84.
Strikemaster Mk 84 '306'; engine fire; crashed into river near Jerantut, Pahang, Malaysia (1), 5-6-73.
Strikemaster Mk 84 '307'; engine failure; crashed into sea near Changi AB, Singapore 9-1-74.
Strikemaster Mk 84 '309'; engine failure; crashed into jungle 17 miles north-west of Kluang, Malaysia 3-8-71.

OMAN 'THE SECRET WAR'

On 1 March 1959, the Sultan of Muscat and Oman's Air Force (SMOAF) was created under the command of former wartime fighter pilot, Sqn Ldr Barry Atkinson; its initial equipment was delivered the same year and comprised Hunting Percival Provost T.52s for the COIN role and Scottish Aviation Pioneer CC.1s. The first seven pilots, who had all been seconded from the RAF, were converted to the Provosts at RAF Manby and eventually arrived at Bait al Falaj airfield near Muscat in August that same year. With the Jebel Akhdar insurrection resolved by 1959, the northern part of the country remained relatively peaceful, with infrastructure and industry being developed, but this served only to incite further discontent in the south where the Jebali considered themselves ignored and neglected.

As the incursions by the communist-backed rebels of the People's Front for the Liberation of the Occupied Arabian Gulf (PFLOAG) intensified following the British withdrawal from Aden, the British Army Training Team (BATT) and the newly renamed Sultan of Oman's Air Force (SOAF) began to take the offensive with their latest acquisitions which included Augusta Bell helicopters, Short Skyvan light transport and BAC Strikemaster strike aircraft.

Originally ordered in 1967, the initial number of 16 Strikemasters were delivered between March and August 1969 and formed the primary establishment of No. 1 (Strike) Squadron at Salalah. **Michael Kelly** had been a QFI on Jet Provosts at RAF Acklington before his appointment as a pilot and flight commander in the Sultan of Oman's Air Force during the period, May 1968 to December 1969:

"In early October 1968 I went to Warton to protest at the late delivery of our Strikemasters and had a few trips with BAC's chief test pilot, Paul Millett. I flew our first aircraft '402' on an air test at Nicosia on 5 March 1969. On 14 March 1969, Nos. '401' and '402' became the first jet aircraft to arrive at Bait al Falaj."

With the formation of the People's Democratic Republic of Yemen (PDRY) in 1967, the frequency of communist guerrilla attacks increased with the intention of overthrowing the sultanate, and it was decided to attack their operating bases in the mountainous region of Dhofar. One of the earliest strikes by the SOAF Strikemasters on the rebel positions was in October 1969, when **Michael Kelly**

Michael Kelly at SOAF HQ. (Michael Kelly)

was awarded the Sultan's Bravery Medal for the following action as described in his citation:

> "On 9 October 1969 B Coy NFR [Northern Frontier Regiment] was returning to its company base at HALUF from Operation Greencap. In view of an earlier contact which revealed several strong groups of enemy in the area, top cover was ordered from two 'Jet Provosts' [Strikemasters].
>
> "Flt Lt Kelly was the leader of this sortie and in order to give maximum support to the ground troops (who had already had one man killed) made several low passes over likely enemy positions, looking for targets to engage.
>
> "Three separate groups of enemy opened accurate automatic fire at his aircraft and OC B Coy NFR immediately informed him that he was under fire. Flt Lt Kelly acknowledged the message and immediately turned to attack the enemy with rockets. During this attack he received two hits, one in the starboard fuel tank and one in the starboard wing.
>
> "Though he knew the enemy fire had been effective, this officer returned to the attack for a second and third time before leaking fuel forced him to leave the target area and return to base. It was later reported that six rebels were killed in this action.
>
> "Flt Lt Kelly's determination to give the ground troops the closest and most effective low-level support in the face of strong enemy opposition is worthy of the highest praise. His action undoubtedly dispersed enemy groups waiting to attack our ground troops and almost certainly saved casualties. He pressed home his attacks without regard for his own safety and his skill and personal example were an inspiration to us all."

As Salalah was the capital city of Southern Oman's Dhofar province, the airfield was developed under RAF control to become the principal location for the control of operations against the rebel insurgents. With the delivery of a second batch of Strikemasters in 1973 the SOAF's assets were dispersed between Bait al Falaj and Seeb maintenance base in the north of the country, with RAF Salalah and the desert landing strip at Midway (later known as Thumrait) in the south.

AVM Les Phipps commanded the Sultan of Oman's Air Force during 1972–1973:

> "In early 1973, as part of the intention to strengthen and develop the air force, the SOAF headquarters moved out of their old premises at the Bait al Falaj airstrip near

Muscat into accommodation at the newly completed Seeb International Airport in Northern Oman; flying out of Bait al Falaj with its short strip and surrounding hills had been exciting to say the least.

"Newly arrived pilots destined for the squadrons having a presence in Dhofar all went through a programme of conversion-to-type and operational training before proceeding to Salalah. For the Strikemaster pilots, live weapons training took place on the Hajar range, not far from Muscat.

"Seeb had been built as both a civil airport and a military airbase, each element sharing the flying facilities of the airfield and with separate operating and support areas. It was also intensely hot but no summer monsoon, and was an ideal location for training. Seeb had been formally opened as an international airport by Sultan Qaboos on 23 December 1973 and was a grand occasion when everybody who was anybody was there. As the concluding item in a flypast of SOAF aircraft there was a formation aerobatic display by a pair of Strikemasters, in which I led Flt Lt Nick Rusling in an eight-minute routine that we were later told had caused the crowds to cheer. It had been nothing special – the usual loops, rolls, pull-ups, low-level orbits and head-on passes. But the Omanis had not seen this sort of thing before in their country."

Stewart Lenton was stationed at RAF Salalah with SOAF in May 1970 as the second in command:

"I flew several sorties with them but not as captain as I was RAF and not SOAF. It was a fascinating period for me as the Oman war was very much being lost. The only road access to Salalah was occupied by the rebels and the sole access was by air or sea. It was not until Sultan Qaboos took over from his father that things started to change. The Strikemaster was a very successful machine especially with the French Sura rocket system, and on 20 September 1970 I was flying with Wg Cdr Hirst when we saw a rebel tribesman shooting at us with a rifle from a hilltop – and after one rocket at him he ceased to exist.

"I also flew with Del Moore (who was sadly killed in a flying accident in July 1972) in the DHC Beaver on one occasion to the wadi [dried river bed] strip of Hawf right on the border with Yemen. Two forts faced each other across the wadi and ineffectual rifle fire was frequently exchanged between them. An approaching thunderstorm hastened us back to the strip but when it came to take off there was a strong crosswind and Del failed to keep the aircraft on the strip. We bounced through rocks and bushes, and I thought my end had come, but we bounced off a rock into the air below take-off speed and somehow stayed in the air. It was a very chastened Del who flew us back and I hardly got a word out of him. I returned to the UK in March 1971."

On 5 May 1972, the PDRY made a surprise attack against Harabut Fort on the border with South Yemen, some 120 miles north-west of Salalah. Two forts faced each other across a narrow wadi; one in Oman manned by the Dhofar gendarmerie, the other in PDRY. A patrol from the local Omani Firqat (a type of local militia) attempted to cross the wadi in the direction of the PDRY and sustained many casualties. This then triggered a mortar and machine-gun attack by the enemy on the Omani fort, and with the Border Crossing Authority (BCA) being approved on 6 May, the SOAF Strikemasters flew two waves against the PDRY fort and a variety of targets over the border, including gun positions and storage areas.

Russ Peart was a pilot with SOAF between 1972 and 1974, flying DHC Beaver and Strikemaster aircraft in some 200 operational sorties against the rebel insurgents; 180 of these sorties involved live firing during which his aircraft was hit many times. He was also wounded by a 75-mm shell when his base was attacked and was evacuated back to the UK:

"I joined No. 1 Squadron at Salalah on 10 January 1972, and my first Strikemaster flight was in the one two-seater (412) we kept at Salalah, together with Bob Ponter, an ex-Fleet Air Arm pilot. My first nine Strikemaster familiarisation flights at Salalah were in that aircraft with other pilots. I then spent time in the north at Bait al Falaj flying the Strikemaster on the range and learning to fly the Beaver. My first operational flight in a single seater was on 27 February in '409'. My logbook just says: 'recce west' … no weapons were used.

"The attack on Harabut in May 1972 was fierce and prolonged, and our soldiers were forced to evacuate the fort and retreat to a wadi for cover. From there they were calling on the radio for assistance, but as the fire was coming from the other side of the border we were in no position to do anything without permission from higher authority. The next morning, 6 May, they were still being pinned down and could not evacuate further. I remember the voice on the HF radio repeatedly saying, 'Please send the jets, please, send the jets'. All of us Strikemaster pilots were ready to go, life jackets on, etc. and it seemed that our senior officers were having to wait on the authority from the sultan.

"Eventually it came. Firstly a Skyvan was sent to drop leaflets over the enemy fort, which proved difficult and the firing and shelling continued. Bill Stoker led a five-aircraft formation and I went along in the right seat with him, the plan being that I would lead the second wave. The first attacks went quite well, two aircraft were hit by ground fire but not too seriously. We felt a loud thump in our aircraft as we recovered into a climb from the first attack with bombs. All the systems seemed OK so we continued with the rocket attack on the fortified position near the fort. The others did much the same. None of our bombs were a direct hit on the fort, but some very near misses did some damage to it and the various adjoining positions. We joined up and returned to Salalah where I found two holes in the tailplane from a 0.5-inch machine-gun round and a smaller 7.62-mm round.

"I led the second wave as planned, but en route we were called to help a unit near the Jinni waterhole. I elected to divert there with my No. 2, leaving Nigel Wilkinson to lead the remaining three aircraft to Harabut. On arriving there, Nigel proceeded to hit the fort, causing serious damage. Later intelligence reports indicated that 12 enemy were killed and 25 wounded, in addition to considerable damage to the fort and to gun and mortar equipment. However, our diversion to Jinni turned out to be a waste of time and a distraction from an important action."

Following the PDRY incursions at Harabut, the sultan ordered the SOAF to attack the enemy installations and weapons at Hawf, just across the border of Yemen. The rules of engagement had been changed after Harabut and seconded pilots were no longer authorised to cross the border as SAF commanders were conscious of the political implications of an RAF officer being shot down over PDRY territory.

The four targets in the town were quite specific as they were in a strip which was referred to as 'alleyway feature'. There were three stores buildings, the front political house and a vehicle-parking area. It was thought that a high-level meeting was due to take place in the political house on or around the date of the strike. The attack by Peter Hulme hit the house with a pair of 540-lb bombs.

Russ Peart again:

"Hawf was attacked because the sultan was furious about the rebel assault on his fort at Harabut. After Harabut I believe questions were asked in the House of Commons and MPs were assured that no serving British pilots had been involved in the cross-border operation. The four buildings at Hawf which were specifically targeted were all used by the Front. The political house and three stores (none of them were ammunition stores), together with a vehicle park were all hit or destroyed. The contract pilots involved were our CO, Sqn Ldr Peter Hulme, Geoff Harding, John Graves, Nev Whittaker and Bob Ponter.

"On 26 May 1972, the contract officers, again led by Peter Hulme carried out a series of attacks against targets in the mountains, destroying stores and equipment, causing many enemy casualties. On the second day, Hulme's aircraft was hit by a 12.7-mm Shpagin bullet. With his radio non-operational, and fuel vapour pouring into the cockpit, Hulme would have been perfectly justified in abandoning his badly damaged aircraft. However, risking imminent fire and explosion, he successfully brought it home. He flew back accompanied by Bob Ponter and was trailing a severe fuel leak from the rear of the fuselage around the jet pipe. He climbed as high as possible and when the engine stopped due lack of fuel he glided to Salalah and did a near perfect glide landing. The aircraft was repaired and Hulme was later awarded the Sultan's Gallantry Medal.

"After three sorties on 8 June, I was with a group of ten enjoying a drink in the evening on the patio outside the officers' mess. The siren sounded a warning of a potential adoo attack on the base, which happened on a fairly regular basis. However, on this occasion, a few seconds after the siren sounded a 75-cm RCL (recoilless launcher) round crashed into the ground just several feet from where we were standing or sitting. We were very lucky as a large metal box on the patio absorbed a great deal of the shrapnel, but Peter Hulme and a RAF air traffic controller, Bill Cooper, suffered extremely serious leg injuries; both were taken to the field hospital, with Bill having to have one leg amputated.

"I remember lying next to another pilot, Taffy Hinchcliff, who had a neat hole in his lower leg. I then stood up and felt a stinging feeling and saw my right boot filling up with blood. I assumed that I had been hit by flying glass, but on inspection I found a deep square hole below my knee cap and felt an inch-long piece of metal with my finger nail. I walked to the field surgical team just as the RAF Regiment were returning fire and was put down in one of the tents while waiting for the medics to deal with the more seriously wounded. In due course I was put on the operating table, and after some time was flown by RAF Hercules to the hospital in Akrotiri. Eventually, after two weeks in Cyprus we were flown to the UK to begin a month's sick leave.

"I was back in a Strikemaster after only nine weeks from receiving the injury and finally returned to Salalah for my next operational sortie on 30 August, attacking several wadis just to the north."

Ian Hawkridge had been based at Seeb for two years working on line maintenance before transferring into the technical control office:

"Seeb was a maintenance and, occasionally, a pilot refresher training base. It was a very interesting place at times, such as when the Iran/Iraq war was on as we were only 30 minutes flying time from Bandar Abbas on the Iranian coast. Unofficially, Iraqi SA-321 Super Frelon helicopters were based with us, alongside an Egyptian air force Tu-16 bomber as Egypt was unofficially helping Iraq. That state of affairs didn't last for too long though as Tehran made it very plain to Oman that if those aircraft failed to be removed, then there would be consequences, so we all breathed a sigh of relief when they departed.

"In 1977 I got the chance to transfer to SOAF Thumrait to start up and operate a Transit Servicing Flight. Thumrait was a challenge for most people as it was located right in the middle of the desert: 360 degrees of sand and not too many facilities to keep you occupied. Airwork had different contracts in many foreign countries. Openly, they provided manpower from ground personnel to pilots for quite a few fledgling air forces, though not officially any actual fighting forces. Any active military personnel that were required were either seconded from the British Army/RAF, etc, or those who had previously resigned their commissions and then re-signed with that particular country's armed forces, as was the case in Oman."

During one such diversionary operation in support of Operation Badree on 19 August 1975, the commander of the SOAF Dhofar Brigade was visiting a SAF position near the border when ten Katyusha rockets struck the position in quick succession. In response, a pair of Strikemasters was called in and attacked the enemy positions to the north of Sherrishitti.

As the Strikemasters turned for home, a Soviet SAM-7 missile was fired from the enemy position and struck the tail of one of the aircraft (406), resulting in the pilot, Flt Lt Roger Furlong, ejecting into the Wadi Jawt. Fortunately, a helicopter was in the vicinity on a re-supply mission and began a search for the downed pilot. Despite intense ground fire and at least one more SAM-7 being launched, which missed its target, the helicopter was able to winch the pilot to safety. These were the first of the latest heat-seeking missiles to be encountered during the conflict, and in all 23 SAM-7s were fired during the operation, accounting for the Strikemaster and a helicopter.

Dennis 'Nobby' Grey had been a Jet Provost QFI at Linton-on-Ouse. From October 1971 until August 1973, he took part in the SOAF Strikemaster and Beaver operations during the Dhofar War, logging over 300 operational sorties. This piece provides a small glimpse of his experiences during that war, based on a paper published in 2010 in the *RAF Historical Society's Journal No. 49*:

"I had heard virtually nothing about Oman and the war in Dhofar until a couple of my flying instructor colleagues were posted there in 1970. A few months later, when my boss at RAF Linton-on-Ouse asked me whether I would be interested in a secondment to the Sultan of Oman's Air Force flying Strikemasters, I jumped at the chance. On offer was a unique operational tour at a time in the middle of the Cold War when there was no other action available for ground-attack pilots. For political reasons, the UK government saw the Dhofar War as a 'Secret War'. Although the SAS, seconded British officers from all three services and ex-officers on contract to the Oman forces were involved in Oman, and British lives were being lost, very few people in the UK knew about the conflict.

"The tour length averaged 18 months to two years. Salalah was an RAF base and OC Salalah was a Royal Air Force squadron leader, the post later being upgraded to wing commander. The ratio of contracted to seconded officers was two to one. At Salalah, SOAF officers lived in the RAF officers' mess and slept in prefabricated air-conditioned rooms surrounded by large oil drums full of sand as a defence against incoming enemy weapons. Strikemaster pilots (some of whom also flew the DHC Beaver) could expect to fly up to two or three operational sorties each day that they were based at Salalah. We normally spent a few days every six weeks in Muscat for training and rest and recuperation.

"After a series of setbacks, the enemy decided to launch a major dramatic attack against government forces and chose the coastal town of Mirbat, some 40 miles east of Salalah airfield. The town was defended by nine members of 'B' Squadron, 22 SAS Regiment led by Capt Mike Kealy, the local firqat (Arab paramilitary group) and about 25 Dhofar gendarmerie soldiers. The SAS in Oman were known as the British Army Training Team (BATT). Between 200 and 250 of the enemy fighters gathered in the hills to the north of the town with the aim of isolating and encircling it for a few hours, killing local town and tribal leaders and departing back into the hills. They originally planned to attack in the dark at 0300 hours under cover of the khareef (low cloud and fog). The adverse weather was to help them later that morning but during the night a thunderstorm on the mountain delayed the enemy's descent and the first exchanges occurred around the Jebel Ali soon after 0500 hours.

"Back at Salalah, as was standard procedure, two armed and fuelled Strikemasters were on standby to scramble. Two of the pilots on standby, Flt Lts Sean Creak and David Milne-Smith, had been alerted and were listening to developments in the SOAF (Tac) operations room. The small unit at Mirbat was under attack but communications were understandably patchy and the size of the enemy force was not yet known. The cloud base at Salalah was 200 to 300 ft and well below normal limits for take-off and therefore operations. However, as the situation developed, it became clear that operational judgement was required. The pilots had been briefed by the BATT team that the Jebel Ali (a feature just to the north of the town) had been taken and it was probable that the enemy had installed a Russian 12.7-mm Shpagin heavy machine gun on the summit overlooking the town. This would be a real threat. Creak led the pair of aircraft in a close formation take-off. En route they discussed weapon options. The squadron had recently carried out loft bombing trials in which the 540-lb bombs were released from low level in a 30-degree climb, allowing the aircraft to escape the bomb debris hemisphere and also avoid flying over the target. The bombs were free fall and unguided (and therefore not very accurate) so would only be suitable for targets away from own troops (like large caves or storage areas). Clearly, loft bombing would not be suitable on the current operation so the option was quickly dismissed. Furthermore, while it is risky firing guns and rockets in very low-level flight, dropping non-retarded ('slick' bombs with no retard parachute) in this situation would be suicidal – the bombs would explode underneath the delivery aircraft. On a routine sortie, Strikemasters would climb to 3,000 ft or so – outside small-arms range – to reconnoitre the area and plan the attack. However, because of the low cloud and the obvious urgency of the situation on the ground, the pilots immediately elected to carry out level strafe and rocket attacks below the cloud. This was an extremely dangerous approach from the pilot's point of view because of the high risk of being hit by one's own ricochets.

"As the pilots approached the target area, they attempted to contact the BATT, without success. Milne-Smith suggested that they try an alternative, commonly used VHF frequency. Contact was established straight away with LCpl Roger Cole who was located in the BATT house. Cole explained that they were under attack from several directions by numerous enemy fighters who were descending from the mountains. Creak was now running in, seconds away from the target area, closely followed by Milne-Smith. Creak asked Cole, 'How close is the enemy?' Cole replied, 'One hundred yards and closing'. Cole said it again. Creak acknowledged and immediately attacked the enemy at ultra-low level as they were clambering over the barbed wire defences of the northern perimeter. The noise of the jets was deafening and, critically, the attack caused the enemy to hesitate. This was the air strike which prevented the 25-pound gun from being overrun and in all probability the battle from being lost. After the first attack, Cole handed the SARBE radio to Cpl Bob Bennett who directed the remaining air strikes from the roof of the BATT house. Creak's aircraft was hit seven times on this first pass by enemy machine-gun fire. With the high probability of an even greater emergency situation developing (fire, fuel leak, engine failure, hydraulic leak) Creak was forced to return to Salalah leaving Milne-Smith to continue the attacks alone. Milne-Smith managed to expend all his 16 SURA rockets and most of his ammunition on the enemy before landing back at Salalah after a one hour and 15-minute sortie with, miraculously, no bullet strikes on his jet. On landing, Milne-Smith was met by the squadron commander, Sqn Ldr Bill Stoker, and they were briefed for the next sortie.

"Milne-Smith led Stoker back to the battle at around 0915 hours. The cloud base had improved only slightly, so, again, no bombs were dropped. In fact, no bombs were dropped on any of these sorties, contrary to some published eyewitness reports which, in the heat of the action, probably confused the rocket explosions with bombs. The two pilots arrived in the area and set up a racetrack pattern, turning right after individual weapons release. With calls of 'inbound' and 'outbound', they managed to avoid a mid-air collision. After their third or fourth pass firing rockets and guns, Stoker's aircraft was hit badly and began losing fuel rapidly from his wing tank. He steered west towards Salalah above the cloud. Milne-Smith carried out a visual inspection and flew in formation with Stoker throughout the recovery and the subsequent precautionary forced-landing pattern (i.e. with the engine fully throttled back). They emerged from the cloud at only 800 ft and Stoker landed without further damage. Miraculously, Milne-Smith's aircraft had once again escaped being hit by any bullets.

"Meanwhile, the SOAF helicopters had been involved from about 0730 hours in evacuating casualties. At around 1030 hours the first SOAF helicopters arrived on the beaches to the south of Mirbat to land 23 fully armed BATT from 'G' Squadron to clear the remainder of the enemy and to collect the wounded. The helicopters, led by Sqn Ldr Neville Baker, were involved in several heroic incidents that day.

SOAF pilots. In the cockpit (L to R): John Wools, Bob Ruskell, and Frank Milligan (boss). Middle row: Dick Thomas, Keith Middleton, and John Spencer. Back row: Stan Hodgkins and Robin Russell. (Stan Hodgkins)

Soon afterwards, when the majority of the fighting was over, I was tasked to provide Strikemaster top cover in support of the mopping-up operations as the surviving enemy withdrew into the mountains. By this time, the cloud was lifting and breaking and I vividly recall the devastation in the area of the fort and how black the cloud was as a result of enemy mortar strikes. Three years after the event, the UK government awarded Sqn Ldrs Stoker and Baker the Omani Distinguished Service Medal for Gallantry, an Omani equivalent of the VC.

"When the Omani victory eventually arrived, some five years later, it had been hard won. Defeat would almost certainly have condemned the Gulf to years of instability and anarchy. In the end, a model counter-insurgency campaign brought about a rare, unambiguous and enduring victory over communism. In retrospect, it could be argued that the campaign fought in Oman had been of potentially greater strategic significance than the concurrent Vietnam War."

Stan Hodgkins:

"As far as I remember it, the final chapter started in October 1975 – the so-called 'Octoberfest', because at the end of the monsoon in October the clouds finally rolled away to reveal the coast of Dhofar transformed with dense vegetation in a brilliant emerald green – the same colour as a can of Heineken. By that time the adoo were confined to western Dhofar, below a scarp (a sheer cliff resembling a giant step).

"The SOAF, under Brig John Akehurst had planned the post-monsoon operation in western Dhofar from Mirbat to the Yemen border for months as the final push to drive the communist rebels and the PDRY troops out of Oman. The monsoon usually forces a pause in any unpleasantness but traditionally things tend to become hot again when it clears away, and on 14 October 1975 the offensive commenced. Descending from the high ground at night, the Muscat Regiment secured the large 'Capstan' rock feature, with very little opposition, and by quickly moving down to the sea, the supply route to South Yemen was cut, trapping the enemy forces. On 17 October, six Strikeys from Salalah led by the CO, Sqn Ldr George Aylett struck adoo positions below the distinctive 'Simba' rock formation from the sea at dawn with guns and SURA rockets. There was considerable return fire but there were no losses and the boys came back with vivid descriptions of spectacular tracer fire. Unfortunately (or fortunately) I was on standby so missed the fireworks."

In January 1976, Sultan Qaboos declared that the war was officially over. However, ground-attack operations continued throughout the rest of the year with several mopping-up operations in the Jebel – mainly providing top cover for helicopters – and was concluded on 14 September 1976, with two waves of Strikemasters attacking rebel fighters in an area to the west of Salalah. This would prove to be the last ground-support operation carried out by the Strike Squadron, and in January 1977 the aircraft transferred to the newly formed Flying Training School at RAF Masirah.

David Milne-Smith was a former MEAF Hunter pilot and QFI before being attached to the SOAF:

"With the war now receding fast the commander of the SOAF (initially Gp Capt [later AVM] Les Phipps and subsequently Gp Capt [later AM] Erik Bennett) was charged with modernising, training and reorganising the air force with the aim of putting Omanis in the driving seat – 'Omanisation'. The traditional task of loan service began to change from manning the front line to more of a training, mentoring and standardisation role. Airwork engineers continued to service the aircraft but RAF loan service ground crews and engineering officers were brought in to advise on, and set up training schemes covering basic and advanced trade training. On the flying side, with the Hunter taking the lion's share of the tactical flying and operating from the newly commissioned base at Thumrait, the Strikemasters were relocated to Masirah (now in Omani Mainstay of the SOAF during the Dhofar campaign, the Strikemaster) where a full-blown FTS was set up. The RAF was now asked to provide QFIs and, together with the existing contract pilots, they were tasked with training the Omanis.

"By the end of 1978 there were 11 Omani pilots in service and there has been a steady output since then. However, with the introduction of the Jaguar and the expansion of the helicopter and transport fleets the demand for pilots exceeded supply. Hence the call for more loan service, which the RAF could not fully meet – partly on availability grounds, since volunteers to serve for up to two years unaccompanied were not exactly arriving in droves – and partly on cost grounds. The RAF could not afford to run light and the overall loan-service budget was becoming increasingly stretched. The shortfall in personnel was often made up from recently retired RAF and RN aircrew, supplemented by others from, for instance, the South African and Rhodesian air forces."

On 1 August 1990, the Sultan of Oman's Air Force was renamed the Royal Air Force of Oman as part of its modernisation and re-equipment programme. This programme also saw the eventual withdrawal of the last operational Strikemasters in November 1999 with their replacement by Swiss-built Pilatus PC-9M turboprop training aircraft.

APPENDIX 1
STRIKEMASTER PRODUCTION AT WARTON

PS.101–112	Mk 80	901–912 Saudi Arabia
PS.113–125	Mk 80	1101–1113 " "
PS.126–129	Mk 81	501–504 South Yemen
PS.130–136	Mk 82	401–407 Oman
PS.137–152	Mk 84	300–315 Singapore
PS.153–157	Mk 82	408–412 Oman
PS.158–163	Mk 83	110–115 Kuwait
PS.164–169	Mk 87	601–606 Kenya
PS.170–175	Mk 83	116–121 Kuwait
PS.301–310	Mk 88	NZ6361–6370 New Zealand
PS.311–318	Mk 89	243–250 Ecuador
PS.319–326	Mk 82A	413–420 Oman
PS.327–336	Mk 80A	1114–1123 Saudi Arabia
PS.337–340	Mk 89	251–254 Ecuador
PS.341–346	Mk 88	NZ6371–6376 New Zealand
PS.347–350	Mk 82A	421–424 Oman
PS.351–354	Mk 89	255–258 Ecuador
PS.355–366	Mk 80A	1124–1135 Saudi Arabia

Ten Strikemaster airframes were transferred from Warton to Hurn in 1979 for final assembly:

PS.367–368	Mk 89	259–260 Ecuador
PS.369–372	Mk 90	141/42/44 Sudan
PS.373–375	Mk 89	261–264 Ecuador
PS.376	Mk 80A	425 Oman

APPENDIX 2
JET PROVOST/STRIKEMASTER DESIGN PROJECTS

With the continued development of the Jet Provost and Strikemaster designs, between 1952 and 1965 the company also produced a number of experimental

Designed to investigate the concept of jet flaps to lower take-off and landing speeds, the Hunting HS.126 research aircraft (XN714) was fitted with a Bristol Orpheus turbo-jet engine, together with an undercarriage and a pneumatic system derived from the Jet Provost. (BAe Systems Heritage Warton-Percival/Hunting Collection)

APPENDIX 2 JET PROVOST/STRIKEMASTER DESIGN PROJECTS

projects based on both aircraft. These projects comprised turbo-prop, swept-wing and COIN designs, including a four-engined VTOL research aircraft based on the Jet Provost (P.94 1955), a four-seat communications Jet Provost T Mk 3 (HS.125 1958), a tandem-seated training aircraft developed from the Jet Provost, with two Rolls-Royce RB145 engines (H.127 1958), a two-seat, swept-wing development (H.140 1961), and a ground-attack Jet Provost T Mk 4/T Mk 52 with a BS Viper engine and weapons hardpoints fitted to the wings (P.164 1964).

The majority of these designs failed to materialise, but in 1982 BAe revived its earlier P.164 project when it was proposed that it would complement the RAF's Hawk advanced trainer. Officially named the 'Eaglet', the basic trainer project was redesigned and shared a large amount of commonality with the Strikemaster, including the front fuselage incorporating side-by-side seating, wings, tailplane and a fully pressurised cockpit. Powered by either a Pratt & Whitney JT15D or Garrett Airsearch turbofan engine, it was suggested that fuel savings would result in a significant reduction in running costs. The design, however, failed to attract official interest.

One of the more successful company design projects to emerge from the drawing board which was loosely based on the Jet Provost, was the Hunting HS.126 research aircraft. Built at Luton and fitted with a Bristol Orpheus turbo-jet engine, together with an undercarriage and a pneumatic system derived from the Jet Provost, the aircraft had been designed to investigate the concept of jet flaps to lower take-off and landing speeds. The prototype (XN714) took to the air from Bedford on 26 March 1963, flown by the chief test pilot, Stan Oliver. Further test flights by the RAE's Aero Flight and wind-tunnel testing at the NASA Ames Research Center in California were able to gather valuable information on handling and performance. In 1972, the aircraft was officially withdrawn and eventually donated to the Aerospace Museum at Cosford in April 1974.

GLOSSARY

A&AEE	Aeroplane & Armament Establishment
ACCS(OR)	Air Council Standing Committee (Operational Requirements)
Adoo	enemy; a guerrilla movement
AGL	Above Ground Level
AOC	Air Officer Commanding
BAC	British Aircraft Corporation
BAe	British Aerospace
BEA	British European Airways
BFT(S)	Basic Flying Training (School)
BS	Bristol Siddeley
CAA	Civil Aviation Authority
CAACU	Civilian Anti-Aircraft Cooperation Unit
CFE	Central Fighter Establishment
CFI	Chief Flying Instructor
CFS	Central Flying School
COIN	Counter Insurgency Aircraft
DME	Distance Measuring Equipment
ETPS	Empire Test Pilots School
FAA	Fleet Air Arm
FAC	Forward Air Control
IF	Instrument Flying
IMC	Instrument Meteorological Conditions
JAFACTSU	Joint Forward Air Control Training and Standards Unit
MDS	Miniature Detonation Cord
MU	Maintenance Unit

GLOSSARY

NAS	Naval Air Squadron
NASA	National Aeronautics and Space Administration
NATO	North Atlantic Treaty Organisation
navex	Navigation Exercise
NFR	Northern Frontier Regiment
OASC	Officer and Aircrew Selection Centre
OCTU	Officer Cadet Training Unit
OTU	Operational Training Unit
PDRY	Peoples' Democratic Republic of Yemen
QFI	Qualified Flying Instructor
RAE	Royal Aircraft Establishment
RAAF	Royal Australian Air Force
RCAF	Royal Canadian Air Force
RCL	Recoilless Launcher
RFS	Refresher Flying Squadron
RIAT	Royal International Air Tattoo
RNEC	Royal Navy Engineering College
RNR	Royal Navy Reserve
RR	Rolls-Royce
SAR	Search and Rescue
SBAC	Society of British Aerospace Companies
SHAR	colloquial term for the Sea Harrier
Strikey	colloquial term for the Strikemaster
SOAF	Sultan Of Oman's Air Force
SOC	Struck off Charge
SoTT	School of Technical Training
TWU	Tactical Weapons Unit
UAS	University Air Squadron
u/t	Under Training
VTOL	Vertical Take-Off and Landing

SELECT BIBLIOGRAPHY

Bagshaw, Decon, Pollock & Thomas, *RAF Little Rissington*, Pen & Sword, 2006
McClen, Don, *Neither by Chance or Fate*, Self-published
McDonald, Wg Cdr Paul, *Winged Warriors: The Cold War from the Cockpit*, Pen & Sword, 2012
Peart AFC WKhM, Sqn Ldr Russell, *From Lightnings to MiGs: A Cold War Pilot's Operations, Test Flying & An Airspeed Record*, Pen & Sword, 2021
Robinson AFC*, Sqn Ldr John B., *Life of Flying*, Self-published
White, Rowland, *Storm Front*, Corgi Books, 2011

INDEX

A&AEE 24, 78
Aermacchi MB-339CB 127–8
Airwork Services Ltd 94, 129, 133–4, 160, 165
Allen, Tim 14, 74–6
Anderson, Andy 14, 100, 101
Arguelles, Capt Fredys (FAV) 136
Arlett, Dan 97
Atcherley, AM Sir Richard 'Batchy' 32, 35
Aylett, George 165

BAC 167 Strikemaster 10–12, 95–6, 138–66, 167–8
  G16-26/G-BIDB 139
  G16-27/G-BIHZ 139
  G27-8 138
  G27-9 138
  Mk 80/80A 11, 140, 147, 167
    903–905 147
    1104/N702MF 99
    1114/NZ605GV 99
    1130 104
    G-RSAF '417' 98
  Mk 81 134, 140, 151, 167
    320–323/501–504 134, 151–2
  Mk 82/82A 140, 151–2, 167
    327–331 151–2
    G-SOAF '425' 98, 139, 168
  Mk 83 140–1, 167
    G-BXFV 96
    OJ1–OJ3 141, 143
    OJ6 141
    OJ7 141
    OJ9 142
  Mk 84 140, 150, 152, 167
    300 153, 167
    303 153
    306–309 153
    314/N72445 99
    N167SM 101
    N2146J 101
  Mk 87 140, 143, 167
    601/G-AYHR/OJ4 96, 143, 145, 146
    602/G-BXFP/OJ5 141, 143, 145, 146
    603–606 142–6
    OJ10 142
  Mk 88 124, 140, 167
    NZ6361/N358FS 99, 125–6, 128–9, 167
    NZ6362/N167BA 99, 126
    NZ6363 125, 128–9
    NZ6364/NZ6364Z 99–101
    NZ6369 126
    NZ6370/N187BA 99, 128
    NZ6371 125–6, 167
    NZ6372/ZK-BAC 103, 126, 129
Baldwin, James 14, 22–3
Barclay, Jim 13, 125–7
Barniz, Capt Germain Antonio Rodriguez (FAV) 136
Bashall, Ian 14, 40–1, 42
Bell, Jeff 14, 96–8
Biafran War 129–30

Blissett, Sub-Lt Mick (RN) 53
Blockey, Robin 59
Blower, Lt Chris (RN) 14, 51–2
Blue Air Training 99–100
Booth, Roy 14, 48–9
Boscombe Down 24, 46, 49, 69, 74, 76, 78, 139
Botswana Defence Force 141–2
Bridge, Derick 14, 141–2
British Aircraft Corporation (BAC) 46, 69
British Army Training Team (BATT) 154, 161–3
Brown, Dave 103, 104
Browne, Greg 65, 66–7
Byron, Bruce 14, 72, 151–2

Cameri, Italy 59
Carnazza, Clive 90
Carr, Steve 14, 74, 75
Carvell, Dudley 108
Central Air Traffic Control School 87
Ceylon 118–23
Champniss, Phil 87
Changi, Singapore 91–3, 151–3
Charles, HRH Prince 80–2
Chiddention, Sean 14, 82–3
China Bay 119–22
Coldicutt, David 14, 73–4
Cole, Roger 162–3
College of Air Warfare, RAF Manby 47
Cooper, Bill 159
Corck, Ron 51

Corkett, Allan 14, 105
Coville, Christopher 84–5
Covington, Bill (RN) 14, 65–7
Creak, Sean 162–3
Croser, Dave 14, 69, 79
Curry, David 143–4

Danks, Eddie 14, 78
Davies, Charles 14, 103
Davis, Lt Carl (RN) 51
Davy, John 14, 107
Dawe, Richard 14, 101–2
Denny, Geoff 39
Dhofar War 153–66
Dijon, France 59, 63
Doyle, Terry 14, 41, 47
Dragon Aviation 101
Drinkell, W.G. 'Bill' 17–19

Eagles, Lt Cdr Dave (RN) 14, 139–40
Eastleigh 7, 143–5
Ecuador 11, 26, 139, 140, 167–8
Edwards, Mike 14, 33
Edwards, Lt Marcus (RN) 72
Evers, Eric 71–2
Exeter 94

Farnborough 17, 29, 35, 40, 42, 43, 45, 46, 64, 139, 140
Femi, Lt Dare Ralph (NAF) 129
Fernandez, Lt (RSAF) 152
Fernando, Chira 120–2
Foo Hee Tim, Lt (RSAF) 152
Foster, Candy 13, 20
Foster, Richard 'Dick' 13, 19, 20–1, 49–50
Fox, Dick 43, 51
Foxley-Norris, Sir Christopher 60
French, Mike 57
Fricker, John 29–30
Frost, Ashley 90
Fuller, Brian 58

Gainey, Keith 93–4
Galyer, John 58
Gardiner, Peter 14, 56
Gibbs, Ivor 72
Giffin, Norman 14, 32–4, 36–7

Gill, Norman 14, 112–13
Gilson, O.L. 19
Ginger, Pete 143
Golden Eagle Flight 80–2
Goodwin, John 36
Grainge, John 106–7
Graves, John 159
Grey, Dennis 'Nobby' 14, 106, 108, 161–4

Hall, Brian 14, 104
Halwood, Ian 14, 113–14
Harabut Fort 157–8
Harding, Geoff 159
Harvey, John 14, 93
Hawkridge, Ian 14, 160
Heames, Chris 98
Heaton, Mark 84–5
Hernandez Martinez, Capt Guillermo (FAV) 136
Hirst, 'Curly' 14, 36, 156
Hoar, Peter 14, 49
Hobkirk, Barry 14, 74
Hodgkins, Stan 14, 31–2, 164–5
Holmes, Roy 91
Hoskins, Brian 14, 62–4
Houser, David 17
Howard, Stevie 14, 83–4
Hulme, Peter 158–9
Hunter, Jim 73
Hunting HS.126 169
Hurn 134, 138–9, 168
Hurst, Gregg 83

Innes, Bob 91–2
Iraq 123–4

Jago, Bill 14, 145
Janatha Vimukthi Peramuna (JVP) 119
Jefford, Jeff 12, 14, 86
Jet Provost Trials Unit (Far East) 91–4
Jet Provost:
 Mk 1 17–19, 22–4, 29, 32, 34, 36–8, 49
  G-AOBU 17, 31
  XD674 17
  XD675 17
 Mk 2 23–4, 31
  G-23-1 26

G-AOUS 26
XD694 22
Mk 3 11–12, 23, 26, 37–9, 41–2, 46, 49, 51, 55, 56, 66, 68, 74, 76, 79, 83, 85, 115, 169
 XM346 37
 XM351 96
 XM377 37
 XM384 108
 XM403 37
 XM453 90, 112
 XM455 90
 XM459/G-BWOT 96
 XM465 108
 XM472 74
 XM477 50
 XM579 88
 XN467 46
 XN468 46
 XN508 74
 XN584 88
 XN629/G-BVEG 115
 XN637/BKOU 98
 XP631 108
Mk 4 11, 40–1, 46–67, 107–8, 115, 133
 G-JETP 96
 XP547/N547XP 89–90, 100
 XP549 47
 XP550 47
 XP558 94
 XP564 89
 XP629 87
 XP653 87
 XP688 87
 XR643 94
 XR646 96
 XR653 87
 XR674 87
 XR679 89–90, 94
 XS177 87, 94
 XS178 89, 90
 XS181 87
 XS219 87, 89, 90
 XS221 91, 93
 XS223 91, 93, 133
 XS224 91–3, 153
 XS228 99, 133

INDEX

Mk 5/5A 10–12, 57, 58, 68–86, 108, 138
  XS230 69
  XS231 69
  XW287/N287XW 70–1, 86, 101–2
  XW288 71
  XW289 73
  XW293 96
  XW295/VH-JPV 102
  XW296 73, 75, 86
  XW297 74–5
  XW298 73
  XW299 73
  XW301 74
  XW304 96
  XW307 86
  XW310 96
  XW312 108
  XW320 13
  XW322 80
  XW323 80, 82–3
  XW324/G-BWSG 96–8
  XW326/N326GV 100
  XW327 13
  XW335 82
  XW336 86
  XW374 82
  XW375 13
  XW428 82
  XW429/N556A 86, 99–100
  XW436 13
Mk 51 117–18, 129–30
  124 130–1
  139 131
  143/NAF701 129
  157/NAF702 129, 131, 167
  162 130
  CJ701 122–3
  CJ702 122
  CJ703 119
  CJ704 118, 122
  CJ705 122–3
  CJ706 120, 122
  CJ707 122
  CJ708 119
  CJ709 122
  CJ710–CJ712 123

Mk 52 99, 117, 123, 130, 134, 151–2, 189
  101/350 133, 151–2, 167
  102/351 133, 151–3
  103 131, 133
  104/352 99, 133, 151–2
  105/353 133, 151
  106/354 133, 151
  107/355 133, 151–2
  108/356 133, 151–2
  E-040–E-054 134–5, 137
  G-PROV 96, 99
Johns, Richard 80–1
Jones, David 14, 54–5

Katunayake, Ceylon 118–21
Kelly, Michael 14, 154–5
Kenyan Air Force (KAF) 143–6
Kenyatta, Jomo 143, 145
Khalafalla, Lt Col Awad (SAF) 131
King Faisal Air Academy (KFAA) 104, 147–9
King, Richard 'Dick' 14, 52–3
Klootwyk, Ares 14, 129–30
Knight, Olly 14, 38–9, 58–60

L-29 Delfin 102, 123–4, 129
Laikipia Airbase, Kenya 145
Lane, Herbert 42
Langworthy, Bill 48, 51
Las Vegas, Nevada 99
Lavender, Danny 14, 131–3
Lenton, Stewart 14, 53–6, 156–7
Liew, Capt Mickey (RSAF) 152
Lloyd, Terry 6–7, 14, 42–5, 143–4
Lokuge, Noel 14, 118
Long, Chris 11–12
Lord, Capt Dick (USAF) 72
Loveday, Pete 93
Luton 11, 16–17, 24–6, 29, 31, 37, 46, 69, 119, 134–5, 169

Maloney, Tom 95
Mann, Erik 14, 148–50
Mariscal Sucre Airbase 136–7
Mayadev, Vijay 14, 124
McCann, David 14, 130
McClen, Don 33, 34–5, 147

McDonald, Paul 14, 67, 84–6
McIntyre, Dave 14, 88–90
Millington, Peter 33
Milne-Smith, David 14, 162–3, 165–6
Moore, Peter 126
Morrice, John W. 17, 19
Muthukrishnan, Kris 14, 119–20
Mwanzia, Maj Larry (KAF) 144–5

Ng, Lt (RSAF) 152
Nice, Brian 42
Nicholson, Alick 14, 74
Nigeria 129–30
Noades, Roger 91
North Wales Military Aviation Service 98–9
North Weald 31, 42, 96, 98–9, 115–16

Ohakea, New Zealand 125–8, 152
Oliver, Stan 29, 46, 169
Ord, George 91
Osborne, Bob 14, 105–6

Packer, Fred 33–4
Pattinson, Ron 14, 57–8
Peart, Russ 14, 157–60
Percival Aircraft Company 16
Percival Provost 8, 10, 16, 19, 49, 153
Perreaux, Euan 57
Pesquera, Dondi 14, 100
Petrie, Mark 14, 98
Phipps, Les 14, 155–6, 165
Ponter, Bob 157, 159
Poole, Lt Cdr David (RN) 76
Poyser, Graham 31

RAAF Butterworth 92–4
RAF display flying teams:
  CFS Jet Aerobatic Team 34
  Cranwell Poachers 58, 78, 82
  Gemini Pair 56–60, 95
  Gin Section 51
  Linton Blades 73, 75, 83, 108
  Linton Gin 51

Red Arrows 45, 49, 57–8, 62–4, 72, 78, 107
Red Pelicans 34, 40–5, 48, 71, 72, 107, 152
The Macaws 62–4, 94
The Redskins 36
Viper Red 108
RAF squadrons and units:
  1 FTS 13, 40, 49–55, 64, 67, 72–8, 83–5
  2 FTS 7, 18–19, 31, 37, 47, 54, 108, 115
  2 Sqn 58, 77
  3 FTS 13, 48, 54, 55–60, 71
  3/4 Civilian Anti-Aircraft Cooperation Unit 94
  4 Sqn 65, 78
  6 FTS 13, 54–5, 79, 86
  7 FTS 13
  27 MU 37, 93
  79 Sqn 87–90
  229 OCU 87
  Central Flying School 7, 11, 13, 21, 23, 32–7, 39, 40, 45, 47, 48, 53, 62, 70–5, 77, 80, 96, 125, 133, 141, 150
  Joint Forward Air Control Training and Standards Unit (JFACTSU) 88–90
  Tactical Weapons Unit (TWU) 47, 66, 88–90
  The College of Air Warfare/ School of Refresher Flying 47, 61–4
RAF stations:
  Abingdon 54–5
  Biggin Hill 45, 114
  Church Fenton 13, 52–3, 58, 64, 82, 96, 148
  RAF College Cranwell 13, 47, 58, 72, 77–8, 80–3, 113–15, 144, 147
  Cosford 13, 35, 87, 90, 97, 169
  Hullavington 8, 18–24, 29, 31, 32, 34, 37, 49
  Leeming 31, 48, 54–7, 62, 66, 75–7, 79, 88, 96, 113, 143–4

Linton-on-Ouse 13, 47, 49–54, 64–5, 67, 72–6, 82–5, 93, 106, 150, 161
Little Rissington 7, 18, 32, 34, 39, 41–2, 47, 58, 70–3, 96, 108, 112, 133, 141, 150
Manby 17, 47, 61–2, 94, 153
St Athan 13, 34, 78, 87, 89
Syerston 37–8, 42, 47, 49, 54, 109–10, 112, 130, 141
Ternhill 12, 45, 131
Valley 42–5, 49, 62, 67, 75–6, 82–3, 106
Republic of Singapore Air Force (RSAF) 151–2
Revell, Gordon 57
Rhind, 'Jimmy' 36
Rigg, Hugh 14, 51
Riyadh 104, 139, 145, 147–9
Robinson, John 14, 58, 70–1, 72–3, 80, 82
Romero, Lt Hector Enrique Segovia (FAV) 136
Royal Ceylon Air Force (RCyAF) 118–23
Royal Navy 49–51, 64–7
  809 Sqn 65, 139
Royal New Zealand Air Force (RNZAF) 124–9
Royal Saudi Air Force 138, 147–50
Ryan, Mick 14, 91–3

Salalah, Oman 154–65
Saudi Arabia 11, 133–4, 138, 140, 145, 147–50, 167
Sedman, Michael 14, 108, 112
Seeb 155–6, 160
Seletar, Singapore 91, 93
Shadbolt, Brian 14, 23
Sheppard, Alan 14, 61–2
Sheppard, Ian 14, 20–2, 36
Singapore Air Defence Command (SADC) 150–1, 153
Slade, Hugh 14, 65–7
South Yemen 118, 133–4, 140, 151, 153, 157, 165, 167
Southern, Dennis 48
Spence, Chris (RAAF) 14, 76–7

Stanton, Steve 14, 147–8
Stevenson, Pete 59
Stock, Reg 14, 37–8, 69, 134–5, 139
Stoker, Bill 158, 163–4
Strikemaster Display UK 98–9
Suckling, Ollie 98
Sudanese air force (SAF) 130–3
Sultan of Oman Air Force (SOAF) 154–66
  Operation Badree 160
Sweetman, John 131
Swift, Ralph 129
Swords Aviation 99

Taylor, Geoff 87
Tengah, Singapore 91–3, 150, 153
Teo, Capt Michael (RSAF) 153
Thompsett, Mike 129–30
Thompson, Bob 14, 58, 95
Thorn, Tim 14, 108–12
Tod, Jonathan 14, 49–51
Turner, Bob 54, 73, 75, 112

Venezuela 11, 26, 118
Venezuelan air force (FAV) 134–7
  'Los Aguiluchos' display team 136
  'Los Escorpiones' 136
Venugopal, Pattathil 15, 28–9, 123

Ward, George 9–10, 16
Wareham, Pat 90
Warren, David 15, 102
Warton 7, 10, 11, 69, 70, 78, 80, 99, 108, 114, 130, 138–41, 143, 144–6, 154, 167
Webb, David 'Duck' 77–8
Webb, John 90
Wheldon, R.G. 'Dick' 17, 25
Whitfield, Joe 15, 144–5
Whittaker, Nev 159
Williamson, Keith 37–8
Wood, Ian 'Iggy' 15, 127–9, 152
Wright Jubilee Trophy 42, 75, 77–8, 82, 94, 108

Yeo, Capt Gary 150